Collins

Get Ready for IELTS

Workbook

Pre-intermediate to Intermediate
IELTS Band 3.5–4.5

Fiona Aish
Jane Short
Rhona Snelling
Jo Tomlinson
Els Van Geyte

William Collins' dream of knowledge for all began with the publication of his first book in 1819.

A self-educated mill worker, he not only enriched millions of lives, but also founded a flourishing publishing house. Today, staying true to this spirit, Collins books are packed with inspiration, innovation and practical expertise. They place you at the centre of a world of possibility and give you exactly what you need to explore it.

Collins. Freedom to teach.

HarperCollins*Publishers*
The News Building,
1 London Bridge Street
London SE1 9GF

First edition 2016

10 9 8 7 6 5 4 3 2 1

© HarperCollins*Publishers* 2016

ISBN 978-0-00-813566-9

Collins® is a registered trademark of HarperCollins*Publishers* Ltd.

www.collinselt.com

A catalogue record for this book is available from the British Library

Authors: Fiona Aish
Jane Short
Rhona Snelling
Jo Tomlinson
Els Van Geyte
Publisher: Celia Wigley
Commissioning editor: Lisa Todd
Editors: Michael Appleton, Helen Marsden
Cover design: Angela English
Typeset in India by Jouve
Printed in Italy by Grafica Veneta S.p.A

Photograph Acknowledgments:
All photos from Shutterstock

p2: Rido; p6: India Picture; p6: anekoho; p6: Andresr; p8: www.BillionPhotos.com; p8: Paul Vasarhelyi; p8: Zurijeta; p8: Ozgur Coskun; p8: JPMediaProductions; p8: Nodokthr; p9: Repina Valeriya; p9: Samuel Borges Photography; p10: Eugenio Marongiu; p10: Joao Seabra; p10: Dragon Images; p10: Ollyy; p10: George Dolgikh; p10: 1970s; p11: auremar; p11: Tanya Uralova; p11: Maridav; p11: mimagephotography; p13: Pressmaster; p13: Ruslan Guzov; p13: Syda Productions; p13: wavebreakmedia; p15: JCREATION; p15: Blend Images; p15: Mikael Damkier; p15: manaemedia; p17: Dragon Images; p17: Geoffrey Kuchera; p17: Melodia plus photos; p19: Celso Diniz; p19: SurangaSL; p19: Elena Elisseeva; p19: Alex Yeung; p21: Sophy Ru; p21: Marina Burrascano; p21: Elnur; p21: Martchan; p22: Pablo Scapinachis; p22: Semmick Photo; p22: Popova Valeriya; p22: Volt Collection; p24: Paul Cowan; p24: zhu difeng; p24: Image Point Fr; p26: SFC; p26: Pavel L Photo and Video; p26: zhu difeng; p26: Racheal Grazias; p26: hans engbers; p26: Paul Matthew Photography; p28: muharremz; p28: daseaford; p28: wavebreakmedia; p28: Monkey Business Images; p30: Ditty about summer; p30: Inga Ivanova; p30: Pics-xl; p30: Konstantin L; p32: StockLite; p33: Maridav; p33: MIKHAIL GRACHIKOV; p33: urbanbuzz; p33: aga7ta; p33: Ditty_about_summer; p33: Stanislav Ratushnyi; p35: LuckyImages; p35: Crystal Home; p35: RTimages; p35: Pressmaster; p37: sdecoret; p37: Photographee.eu; p42: Dabarti CGI; p42: Denys Prykhodov; p42: bikeriderlondon; p42: Alex Mit; p46: Galyna Andrushko; p46: Pikoso.kz; p46: hessbeck; p46: stocker1970; p48: gualtiero boffi; p48: wavebreakmedia; p48: Zurijeta; p48: Goodluz; p54: Oleksiy Mark; p54: CLS Design; p54: wavebreakmedia; p54: Ollyy; p56: Toranico; p56: auremar; p56: Pressmaster; p56: Studio10Artur; p58: Goodluz; p58: michaeljung; p58: Nicolaas Weber; p58: wavebreakmedia; p62: manzrussali; p64: Max Topchii; p64: kaczor58; p64: Alexander Ishchenko; p64: Judex; p70: XXLPhoto; p70: PRILL; p70: PhotoSky; p70: Riccardo Piccinini; p73: NRT; p73: Skylines; p73: Serg64; p73: Gyorgy Barna; p74: Ollyy; p74: Monkey Business Images; p74: wavebreakmedia; p74: wong yu liang; p77: Tribalium; p77: C-You; p77: imaged.com; p77: MrGarry; p78: Aila Images; p78: Rob Hainer; p78: Ingvar Bjork; p78: Monkey Business Images; p82: ambrozino; p82: gpointstudio; p82: Capricorn Studio; p82: carroteater; p84: Tyler Olson; p84: ZouZou; p84: Tom Wang; p84: Valeriy Lebedev; p86: Robert Kneschke; p86: Minerva Studio; p86: vlad.georgescu; p86: Rido; p88: Monkey Business Images; p88: Minerva Studio; p88: LuckyPhoto; p88: Albert Pego; p89: mekCar; p89: Bloomua; p89: Sandra Cunningham; p89: anatolypareev; p92: michaeljung; p93: Viacheslav Nikolaenko; p93: Frank11; p93: jason cox

Contents

Unit 1 Family

Speaking   Talking about the family

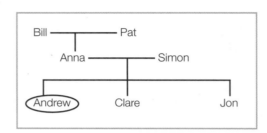

1 Look at Andrew's family tree. Complete the sentences with the words below.

> brothers   daughter   grandparents   husband   mother   parents   sister   sons   wife

1 Clare is Andrew's ....

2 Andrew and Jon are Clare's ....

3 Andrew's .... are called Simon and Anna.

4 Anna is Andrew's .... and Simon's ....

5 Simon and Anna have three children – one .... and two ....

6 Pat and Bill are Andrew's .... Bill is Pat's ....

2 Read and complete the text about Andrew's family.

My name's Andrew. I've got one (1) ....
Her name's Clare. I've got one (2) ....
His name's Jon. He's a student. My (3) .... 's
name is Anna and she's a teacher. My (4) .... 's
name is Simon and he's a doctor.

Watch Out!

Use the contraction **'s** in spoken English.
My name's Andrew.   ~~My name is Andrew.~~

3 Rewrite the text in Exercise 2 to describe your family.

Pronunciation: /ð/

01 **4** Listen and repeat each word. The words below use the phonetic alphabet. This shows you how to pronounce the words. Can you pronounce the /ð/ sound?

brother /'brʌðə/   father /'fɑːðə/   grandfather /'grændfɑːðə/

02 **5** Listen and repeat each word. Then listen again and write the words.

/'brʌðə/ ....   /'mʌðə/ ....   /'grændmʌðə/ ....

Vocabulary: Describing people

6 Find nine personality adjectives below. Use your dictionary to help you. Which adjective describes you?

bossy calm clever confident creative friendly funny happy kind

7 Complete the descriptions with personality adjectives from Exercise 6.

1 My mother understands new things quickly. She's very ....

2 My father is very .... He tells me what to do every day.

3 I'm .... because I believe in my ability. For example, I'm good at speaking English!

4 My sister is never angry or worried. She's always ....

5 My brother is .... He enjoys meeting people. He's .... too. He always makes people laugh.

8 Listen to three people describing someone in their family. Write the personality adjectives that each speaker uses.

Speaker 1: ....

....

Speaker 2: ....

Speaker 3: ....

....

9 Listen again. Complete the sentences with the words you hear. Use the audio script on page 89 to check your answers.

Speaker 1: She .... like her sister. They've both got curly hair.

Speaker 2: I don't have any .... or sisters. I'm an only child.

Speaker 3: But their son is really funny! He's my .... cousin.

10 Describe someone in your family. Use personality adjectives and include extra information.

Grammar: Possessive adjectives

11 Read Anthony's answer to a question about his family. Listen and complete the sentences with the words you hear.

My family? Well, we're a big family, actually. (1) .... house is large! I've got five brothers. (2) .... names are Carlos, Gino, Luca, Alex and Marco. Carlos is 14 and he's the youngest. He's good-looking and very funny. Marco is 27 and he's the oldest. (3) .... wife teaches at my college. (4) .... name is Maria.

My mother is an only child, so (5) .... family is very small. But (6) .... father is from a big family. He has three brothers. He looks like his brother, my uncle Georgio. They are both bossy but kind. My uncle has four children and one cat. (7) .... name is Lola.

Tell me about (8) .... family.

Watch Out!

look like = have the same appearance
I look like my mother.
He looks like his father.
They look like their father.

12 Complete the table.

	you	he		it		they
my			her		our	

13 **Answer the questions. Write full sentences.**

1 Do you have any brothers or sisters?
What are their names?

Example: Yes, I have two sisters.
Their names are Ela and Liz.

2 What is your father's name?

3 Who do you look like in your family?
What is his/her name?

4 Have you got a pet? What is its name?

5 Who makes you laugh in your family?

6 Is someone in your family bossy?

14 **Add one more sentence to your answers in Exercise 13.**

Example: *1 Yes, I have two sisters. Their names are Ela and Liz. Ela looks like my mother and they are both very kind.*

15 **How would you describe your family? Record your answer.**

Listening — Doing a presentation

1

2

3
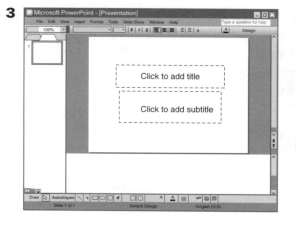

4
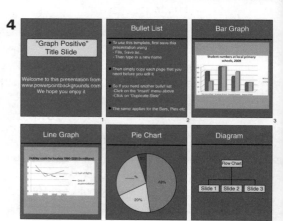

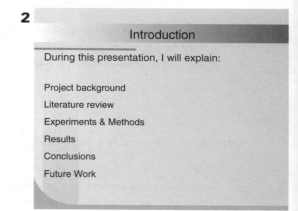

1 The pictures on page 4 show four different stages in organizing a slide presentation. Match the stages below with each image.

a ....

b ....

c ....

d ....

2 Listen to the words below and underline the part that is stressed in each one. The first one has been done for you.

1 intro<u>duce</u>   intro<u>duc</u>tion

2 presentation   present (v)   present (n)

3 suggest   suggestion

4 project (v)   project (n)   projector

5 inform   information

6 explain   explanation

3 Listen to a short conversation and underline the word you hear in each pair of words below. You will hear them in the same order.

1 introduce / introduction

2 suggest / suggestion

3 present (v) / present (n)

4 project (v) / project (n)

5 inform / information

6 explain / explanation

Vocabulary groups

4 It is useful to sort words into vocabulary groups when they refer to the same kind of information, e.g. *female – woman – lady – mother.* Write the words that have a similar meaning in the correct group.

area	bad points	benefits	~~chart~~	cons	dangers
points	graph	icon	image	issue	photograph
good	plan	pros	table	theme	topic

diagram: *chart* ....

picture: ....

subject: ....

advantages: ....

disadvantages: ....

Reading

Family structures

A   B   C

1 **The photos show three different types of family. Match the photos with the words.**

single-parent family ....   extended family ....   nuclear family ....

2 **Complete the three descriptions with a family type from Exercise 1.**

A Greg

Our family is a typical .... There's me, my wife, Sue, and our three children, Adam, Tessa and Tony. We're from Scotland but we live in London – we moved here for work. One of the disadvantages is that the boys don't see much of their grandparents or their cousins, except for when we go to Scotland during the school holidays.

B Benjy

It isn't easy being a .... I got divorced five years ago and now it's just me and the kids. My ex-wife got a new job and moved to Australia. She stays in touch with the children and sends money, but she isn't here to help me bring them up, and my parents live abroad so they can't help.

C Beatriz

We have a big house in the south of the country. It's divided into three apartments: one for my parents, one for my brother and his wife, and one for me, my husband, and our two children. Living in an
.... is very convenient. My brother and his wife are often away but there's always someone to talk to and discuss problems with, or to help with childcare and we save money by sharing things and helping each other.

Watch Out!

Don't waste too much time on unknown words in texts: sometimes you don't need them. When it is useful, try to guess the meaning from the context and make a note of it so you can check it in a dictionary.

3 Match the words 1–12 with the definitions a–l.

1	husband	**a**	two people who are married or in a romantic relationship
2	wife	**b**	a woman who marries one's father after the death of one's mother or after one's parents divorce
3	sibling	**c**	a marriage arranged by the parents of the bride and groom
4	stepmother	**d**	a relative by marriage
5	divorcee	**e**	a person who is divorced
6	in-law	**f**	the male partner in a marriage
7	household	**g**	a woman whose husband has died / a man whose wife has died
8	couple	**h**	all the people of approximately the same age, regarded as a group
9	arranged marriage	**i**	a religious or legal ceremony where two people get married
10	wedding	**j**	the female partner in a marriage
11	widow (f) / widower (m)	**k**	the people who live together in a house
12	generation	**l**	a person's brother or sister

4 Decide if the words below refer to females, males or either.

brother	divorcee	husband	mother-in-law	parent
sibling	son-in-law	stepchild	widow	wife

Female	Male	Either
	brother	

5 Choose the correct words to complete the sentences.

1 Our neighbour, Mr James, is a *husband / divorcee / widower*. His wife died three months ago.

2 I married my *husband / sibling / son* in 2013.

3 Mhairi and James are the young *widows / generations / couple* who live in the apartment downstairs.

4 There are four people in the *couple / marriage / household*: Mr and Mrs Jones and their two children, Alan and Jenny.

5 Mo and Raziye had *a tidy / an ordered / an arranged* marriage.

6 'How many *stepchildren / siblings / parents* have you got?' 'I've got two older sisters and a younger brother.'

7 'Do you get on with your *step-parents / parents / parents-in-law*?' 'Yes, my wife's mum and dad are really nice.'

8 Stephan and Ana are my *in-laws / stepchildren / siblings*. They're my wife's children from her first marriage.

Family and society

1 **Complete the sentences about the family tree by putting the letters in bold in the correct order to form the missing words.**

1 Jon's **o e r m h t** .... is Susan.

2 Jon and Rachel's **o n s** .... is Jason.

3 Jon and Rachel's **u g r e d a h t** .... is Polly.

4 Polly and Jason's **t e r f h a** .... is Jon.

5 Polly and Jason's **e r r a m g o t n d h** .... is Susan.

6 Rachel's **o m e t r h – n i – a w l** .... is Susan.

7 Howard and Susan's **n g n o s a r d** .... is Jason.

8 Jason and Polly's **r n s p e a t** .... are Rachel and Jon.

2 **Read the speech bubbles. Then complete the gaps below with the words in bold.**

My name is Clare and I'm 15 years old. I go to school and this year I **will** have my first exams. I want to be a doctor, but it's difficult to get a place at university, so I **mustn't** fail my exams. To be a doctor, I **must** have a lot of qualifications, but I **don't need to** be very good at art or languages, just science.

I'm Clare's mother, Molly. Clare wants to be a doctor when she's older. I think she **needs to** study hard for this. She plays on her computer quite a lot, which she **shouldn't** do. I think she **should** study more. She's clever. I think she **might** be a doctor.

1 ____will____ – used to talk about something expected in the future
2 _____ / have to / need to – used to say that something is necessary
3 _____ – used to say something is a good idea
4 _____ – used to say something isn't a good idea
5 _____ – used to say it isn't necessary to do something
6 _____ / can / could – used to say that something is possible
7 ____mustn't____ – used to say that something isn't allowed

3 **Rewrite the sentences using the correct modal and semi-modal verbs in Exercise 2.**

1 It is a good idea for children to respect their parents.
   Children should respect their parents.
2 I plan to go to university in the future.
3 It is not a good idea for parents to smoke near their children.
4 It is possible that children will have lessons on the Internet in the future.
5 It is necessary for all children to learn basic skills like maths and reading.

4 **Use modal and semi-modal verbs to give your opinions about events in the future.** *Should, shouldn't, can, might* **and** *could* **are less definite than** *will, need to, must* **and** *have to*. **Compare:**

'Your father will punish you if you don't eat your food,' Fiona's mother said. (= a definite future action)
'You should punish children who disobey their parents,' said George. (= a suggestion)
'Your mum might punish you if you get home late,' Anna told her friend. (= a possibility)

Rewrite the sentences to make them less definite.

1 Children who don't study will fail their exams. (→ a possibility)
2 University must prepare people for good jobs. (→ a suggestion)
3 Children need to follow their parents' advice. (→ a suggestion)

Unit 2 Leisure

Listening — Hobbies, sports and interests

1

2

3

4

5

6

1 **Look at the pictures. Copy and complete the table with the numbers of the pictures and the names of the activities.**

Hobbies	Interests	Sports

Read the vocabulary note and check your answers.

Vocabulary note

A hobby is an activity you do for pleasure in your spare time. It often involves doing something with your hands or collecting something. For example, painting and collecting stamps are hobbies.

A sport is a game that involves physical activity.

An interest is something you enjoy doing. It may be a hobby or a sport, but not always. For example, going to the cinema is an interest, but it is not a hobby or a sport.

Watch Out!

Think about word groups when you do a listening exercise. If you know that a word belongs to a group of words, it is easier to predict what you are going to hear in the recording. For example, if you know that *stamp collecting* is a *hobby*, you will be ready to listen for other words connected with hobbies.

2 **Put the words below in the correct column. Remember: hobbies and sports are interests, but not all interests are hobbies or sports.**

| cooking | football | gardening | going to art galleries | listening to music |
| painting | playing chess | running | swimming | travelling |

Hobbies	Interests	Sports
stamp collecting	going to the cinema	cycling

 3 You will hear some people talking about what they are planning to do in their free time. Write the activity next to the speaker in each conversation. Check that your spelling is correct. Use only one word for each answer.

Conversation A
Speaker 1: *swimming*
Speaker 2: *running*

Conversation B
Speaker 1: ....
Speaker 2: ....

Conversation C
Speaker 1: ....
Speaker 2: ....

Conversation D
Speaker 1: ....
Speaker 2: ....

4 Complete the sentences with the correct word, *to*, *too* or *two*.

1 Michael wants .... go travelling in the vacation.

2 Jeremy has .... much work to do.

3 Annie has .... sisters in Germany.

4 Edward is .... lazy to study for his exams.

5 Elizabeth would like to go .... Paris for the summer.

6 Faizal is planning .... vacations this year.

Watch Out!

Spelling is important in the Listening test. Remember that some words sound the same but are written differently, for example *to*, *too* and *two*. When you hear these words, you will have to think about which one is grammatically possible.

Speaking   How we relax

Vocabulary: Free time activities

A   **B**   **C**   **D**

1 Match the photos A–D with four of the activities below.

chatting online   going shopping   jogging   listening to music
playing computer games   playing tennis   reading magazines   watching a film

2 Complete the table with the nouns below. How many activities can you make?

> a DVD   exercise   football   for walks
> nothing   tennis   to the gym   TV

doing	
going	
playing	
watching	

3 What do you think about the activities in Exercises 1 and 2? Write each activity next to an adjective. Can you add any more activities?

1 boring *doing nothing*
2 relaxing
3 interesting
4 exciting

4 Write sentences for each activity in Exercises 1 and 2. Use *I like … / I don't like …* and an adjective from Exercise 3.

Example: *I don't like playing computer games. I think it's very boring.*

Vocabulary: Expressing preferences

5 Listen to three people answering the question 'What do you like doing in your free time?' What does each speaker enjoy doing? Complete the table with the activities below.

> doing nothing   going for walks   going shopping
> playing computer games   reading magazines   ~~using the Internet~~

Speaker 1	Speaker 2	Speaker 3
using the Internet		

6 Listen to extracts from the answers in Exercise 5. Complete the sentences with the phrases below.

> I don't like   I love   I prefer   I really like
> It depends   My favourite thing

1 .... using the Internet.
2 .... chatting online with him.
3 .... doing nothing to doing exercise.
4 .... going to the gym.
5 .... Sometimes I like going for walks.
6 .... is going shopping.

Watch Out!

We can use **really** + verb to give emphasis. We cannot use **very** + verb.

I really like going to the cinema.
~~I very like going to the cinema.~~

7 Write a short answer to the question 'What do you like doing?' Use the phrases from Exercise 6 and the audio script on page 89 to help you.

Grammar: Present simple

8 **Read the rule and look at the table. Use the information to choose the correct answer, a or b, to questions 1–5.**

- Use the present simple to make general statements about your life.

	+	–
I	like	don't like
You	like	don't like
He / She / It	likes	doesn't like
We / You / They	like	don't like

1 Does your best friend play tennis?
   a No, he doesn't play tennis, but he likes playing computer games.
   b No, he not play tennis, but he likes playing computer games.

2 Do you watch DVDs?
   a Yes. I likes watch DVDs at the weekend. But I don't like watching TV.
   b Yes. I like watching DVDs at the weekend. But I don't like watching TV.

3 Tell me about something you like doing.
   a I liking go to museums. It's very interesting.
   b I like going to museums. It's very relaxing.

4 Do you do any exercise?
   a Yes, I go to the gym every morning at 6 a.m.
   b Yes, I going to the gym every morning at 6 a.m.

5 Do you like reading newspapers?
   a It depends. Sometimes I read the newspapers on Saturdays.
   b It depends. Sometimes I liking the newspapers on Saturdays.

9 **Answer the questions in Exercise 8 about you.**

Watch Out!

on + day: *on Saturdays*
at + time: *at 6 a.m.*
at + the weekend: *at the weekend*
Use **every** to say how often you do something: *every morning*

Reading   Spending time with friends

1

2

3

4

1 **What do we need friends for? Match the words with the pictures. The first one has been done for you.**

chatting	having fun	partying	sharing

1 *partying*
2 ....
3 ....
4 ....

2 Words ending in *-ing* are often at the beginning and at the end of sentences. Complete the sentences with words from Exercise 1.

1 It is difficult for young children, but they have to learn that friendship is about

....

2 .... with friends is not something I do very often, but we always celebrate our birthdays.

3 .... with friends is one of my favourite ways to spend an afternoon. We have so much to say that we often talk for hours.

4 Even on bad days, being with my best friend means ....

Watch Out!

Some verbs have similar meanings, but they are not always interchangeable; it depends on the context. For example, we *spend time* with friends, or more formally, we *socialize* with them; more informally, we *hang out* with them.

3 Which nouns go with which verbs? Copy and complete the table. Then answer the questions below.

~~basketball~~   boardgames   cards   chess   dancing   exercise   hiking   karate   kickboxing
puzzles   shopping   skiing   snakes and ladders   sports   swimming   tennis   weightlifting   yoga

Play	Go	Do
basketball		

1 Which verb do you use most with activities ending in *-ing*?
2 Which verb do you use most for competitive games?
3 Which verb do you use most for other recreational activities?

4 Read about how these people have fun. Underline the words that refer to activities and circle the words that refer to places. Don't use a dictionary yet.

Jack, 15:
I spend time with my family most evenings. At the weekend, I prefer to hang out with my friends at the park or in the playground in the local woods. If it rains, I like to go to see a film with my friends.

Monica, 18:
I belong to a chess club that meets twice a month, and once a year we go camping. It's the highlight of my summer! We stay in tents on a lovely camp site and have picnics and barbecues. In the evenings, we organize quizzes and play cards. And we also play a lot of chess, of course!

Amrita, 12:
My older sisters spend a lot of time with their friends in the local shopping centre, but I'm not allowed to go out without an adult yet. I can still chat to my friends all the time, though, by phone, email or text message.

5 **Find words in the texts in Exercise 4 that have the meanings below.**

1 .... : a large place where you can buy many different things

2 .... : a person who is no longer a child

3 .... : a place where you can stay in a caravan or a tent

4 .... : a meal in the open air

5 .... : outdoor parties where people cook and eat food

6 .... : games in which you have to answer questions

Writing   Trends and statistics

1 **Look at the pictures of hobbies. Then complete the sentences with a verb + noun.**

Gabrielle: I have lots of hobbies. Every weekend I (1) _____*play golf*_____ with my father. There's a club nearby, so we go there. It's really good fun, but it's much better being on the course if the weather is nice and sunny. My father is a better player than me. I usually take four or five shots to get the ball in the hole. In the evenings I (2) .... a lot. I especially like dramas and reality shows.

Yuan: I like sports quite a lot. I (3) .... three times a week! There's a pool near my house, so I usually go there before school. I really love it! I also (4) .... a lot. My favourite singers are Justin Bieber and Miley Cyrus. I use my headphones at home because my mother doesn't like the loud noise!

2 **Put the hobbies below in the correct column. (Some hobbies may be used with more than one verb.)**

| computer games | football | golf | gymnastics | ~~horse riding~~ | karate | shopping |
| skating | sports | swimming | the guitar | the violin | TV | yoga |

Do	Go	Play	Watch
	horse riding		

3 We use the present simple to describe repeated or regular activities.

*I **play*** (present simple) ***football*** (activity) *every week*.

We also use the present simple to talk about things we *like / don't like / love / hate*. These verbs can be followed by another verb in the -ing form.

*I **like*** (*like* verb) *go**ing*** (-ing form) *swimming*.

Complete the text using the present simple tense or the -ing form.

I asked all the people in my class about their hobbies and this is what I found out. Most people in the class like (**1**) *playing* tennis. Julia and Pamela (**2**) _____ tennis four times a week, and Peter (**3**) _____ tennis three times a week. Over half my class (**4**) _____ tennis every week. Brian doesn't like (**5**) _____ tennis. He never plays! The most popular hobby is playing computer games. Nearly everyone (**6**) _____ computer games. Four people (**7**) _____ computer games every day. Only Ellen (**8**) _____ computer games. She thinks they are boring. Half of my class like playing football. John and Paul (**9**) _____ football every day, and Arnold (**10**) _____ football four times a week. Two girls (**11**) _____ football.

	Boys					Girls		
	Arnold	Peter	John	Paul	Brian	Ellen	Julia	Pamela
Football	x4 a week		every day!	every day!		x2 a week		
Tennis	x2 a week	x3 a week	x2 a week		Never!		x4 a week	x4 a week
Computer games	every day	every day	every day	x2 a week	x3 a week	Never!	x2 a week	every day
Swimming						x3 a week	every day	

4 **There are many different words to describe quantity. Put the words below in the correct order from 0 (the smallest amount) to 100 (the largest amount).**

| a lot of   ~~all~~   few   no   not many   not much   some |

0 _____ *all* 100

5 **Look at the information in the table in Exercise 3 and complete the sentences with the correct quantity words.**

1 _____*A lot of*_____ boys like football.
2 _____ the students have at least one hobby.
3 _____ boys like swimming.
4 _____ students play tennis.
5 _____ students go swimming.

Unit 3 Different cultures

Speaking — Celebrations

Vocabulary: Celebrations

A

B

C

1 **Look at the photos of celebrations. Which of the things below can you see?**

> balloons   cake   cards   carnival   costume   family
> fireworks   friends   parade   presents   traditional food

2 **Complete the descriptions of celebrations with the words below.**

> family   give   make   presents

In my country, we celebrate name days.
We (**1**) .... cards and
(**2**) .... traditional food.
I enjoy visiting my (**3**) ....
on my name day and I love receiving
(**4**) ....!

> fireworks   parade   watch   wear

New Year is a very special occasion. There's
a (**5**) .... through the streets
and people (**6**) .... beautiful
costumes. We (**7**) .... the
parade and we celebrate the start of a new
year with (**8**) ....

Vocabulary: Connecting ideas

 3 **Read the description of Steven's trip. Put a–f in gaps 1–6. Then listen and check.**

a   It was a special trip for me **because**

b   **but** it wasn't very nice.

c   it was very exciting!

d   My best friend went **too**.

e   **Then** we visited another city

f   we walked to the city centre.

Last year I travelled to Rio and visited my cousin
and his family. (**1**) .... We went to my
cousin's house and we had a delicious traditional
meal. **After** we ate dinner, (**2**) ....
When we saw the carnival, (**3**) ....
We danced and sang. We watched the
parade. It was fun, but we were very tired.
(**4**) .... and stayed at a famous hotel,
(**5**) .... We stayed for two days and
then we went home. (**6**) .... I travelled
without my parents for the first time.

4 **Look at the bold words in Exercise 3. Then choose the correct word to complete the sentences.**

1 I enjoyed the parade and the carnival, *but / because* I was very tired.

2 We went to a local restaurant for lunch and *then / but* we went to visit some friends.

3 I got a present from my parents. I got a present from my brother *after / too*.

4 *After / When* the graduation ceremony, my family met my friends from university.

5 I didn't enjoy the trip *too / because* I don't like travelling by bus.

6 *When / But* the fireworks started, we were very excited.

Grammar: Past simple

5 **Read the rules and look at the table. Complete the past simple form of the irregular verbs below. Use your dictionary to help you.**

- Use the past simple for past actions that are finished.
- For regular verbs, add *-d* or *-ed*.
- For irregular verbs, learn the different forms.
- For the verb *be*, learn the different forms for *I, you, he/she, we* and *they*.

	Infinitive	Past simple +	Past simple –
Regular verbs	dance	danced	didn't dance
Irregular verbs	sing	sang	didn't sing
The verb *be*	be	was / were	wasn't / weren't

1 eat ....
2 give ....
3 make ....
4 meet ....
5 wear ....
6 see ....

6 **Complete the sentences with the words below.**

> danced   didn't stay   graduated
> was   went   were

1 I wasn't at the carnival. I .... to my sister's wedding.

2 I .... last year. My parents came to England for the ceremony.

3 People wore colourful costumes. It .... an exciting day!

4 We watched the parade. We sang and .... to the music.

5 I stayed with my friends. I .... in a hotel.

6 We didn't see the fireworks. We .... tired and went to the hotel.

Pronunciation: Past simple verbs and -ed

 7 **The *-ed* ending is pronounced in three different ways. Listen to the different sounds and the past simple verbs in the table below.**

/t/	/d/	/ɪd/
danced	stayed	hated
watched	travelled	visited

 8 **Listen to six past simple verbs and add them to the table in Exercise 7.**

Watch Out!

The *-ed* ending adds a sound to the end of a verb. Sometimes it adds an extra syllable.

For example:

dance + *-ed* = *danced* (one syllable)

hate + *-ed* = *ha-ted* (two syllables)

9 **Complete the sentences with the words below. Use the correct form of the verbs.**

> but   meet   travel   watch

I (**1**) .... my friends in the park after the carnival. We (**2**) .... the fireworks and (**3**) .... home. We had a great time, (**4**) .... we were very tired.

> see   play   wear   when

My hometown has a big festival each year. Last year, I (**5**) .... a costume and (**6**) .... traditional music at the parade. My parents were very happy (**7**) .... they (**8**) .... the parade.

Reading   British culture

1 **Quiz: Match these names of buildings in London with their descriptions.**

1 City Hall

2 The Old Bailey

3 The Gherkin

4 The Palace of Westminster

a This building is also known as London's Central Criminal Court or Justice Hall, and was named after the road it was on.

b This is the building where the two Houses of Parliament of the United Kingdom, the House of Lords and the House of Commons, are based.

c This building is home to the Mayor of London and the regional administrative authority, consisting of over 600 members of staff. It is located near the River Thames, where it contrasts strongly with more traditional looking buildings.

d This is an office building at 30 St Mary Axe. It got its name because it is shaped like a vegetable.

2 **Label the pictures with the names of the buildings in Exercise 1.**

1 ....   2 ....   3 ....   4 ....

3 **Look at the words below. Read the text and try to work out which words fit in the gaps. Try to do this without looking at your dictionary.**

> butter   cup   customs   tearoom   jam   kettle   milk   salmon   sandwiches   teapot

In England, 'Put the (**1**) .... on' is a phrase heard often, as people enjoy stopping for a (**2**) .... of tea and perhaps a biscuit. This daily ritual becomes much more formal in a (**3**) .... or hotel setting. If you go out for cream tea, you may get loose tea, brewed in a (**4**) .... and served at your table. This is accompanied by scones with cream and (**5**) .... There are different regional (**6**) .... about how cream tea is served. In Devon, they tend to put the cream on the scone first, with strawberry jam on top, whereas in Cornwall they spread (**7**) .... on the scone first and put the jam on before the cream. A traditional afternoon tea would also be accompanied with delicate (**8**) ...., such as cucumber, egg, ham and smoked (**9**) ...., as well as cakes. However you choose to accompany it, remember that in England, ordinary tea is always drunk with (**10**) ....

4 Copy and complete the table by writing the words below in the right categories. Use a dictionary or check the meanings in the Answer key.

> Cornish pasty   barley water   duck-duck-goose   scones   haggis
> hopscotch   Irn-Bru   rarebit   leek   British bulldog

Food	Drink	Activity

5 Two items in Exercise 4 are typically associated with Scotland, two with Wales and two with England. Which ones are they?

Scotland	Wales	England

Watch Out!

Do you know the difference between the United Kingdom, England, Great Britain and the British Isles? Which ones include Scotland and Wales? If you don't know, you may misunderstand exactly what an author is writing about. You could also cause offence to people in certain areas by using the wrong word! Check the Answer key to Exercise 6 if you are confused.

6 Identify the following on the map:

- England
- Scotland
- Wales
- Northern Ireland
- Ireland
- Republic of Ireland
- Great Britain
- the UK

Cultures across the world

 1
 2
 3
 4

1 **Use the pictures above and the clues to complete the word puzzle.**

Across:

3 This woman is wearing her .... costume.

4 In some villages around the world, people still live in .... like these.

Down:

1 This is an example of .... writing.

2 This is the national food of ....

2 **Check the meaning of the words in the word maps in a dictionary. Then complete the word maps with the words below.**

scarf   vegetarian   spicy   pronunciation   silk   brick   block of flats   alphabet

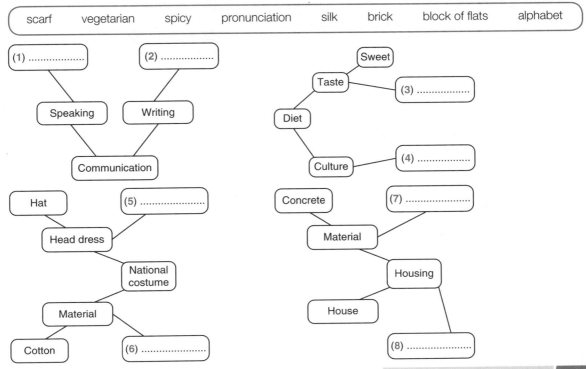

Listening for key words

 3 You will hear four conversations between students discussing their projects on world cultures. Circle the topic of each conversation.

A language, dress, housing, diet

B costume, housing, culture, literature

C clothes, festivals, homes, communication

D communication, food, costume, art

 4 Listen again and in your notebook write any words from the word maps that are mentioned.

5 The verbs *make*, *have* and *do* are often confused. Choose the correct words to complete the sentences.

1 Every year in April we *make / have / do* a Water Festival.

2 Recently, our country has *made / had / done* progress in improving education.

3 In some places tourism has *made / had / done* a lot of damage to the environment.

4 Global warming has *made / had / done* a negative effect on many rare animals.

5 In the spring, we *make / have / do* a lot of work in the garden.

6 When people get married, they *make / have / do* a big party to celebrate.

Writing

Culture

A

B

C

D

1 Label the pictures with the words below. Then complete definitions 1–4.

> architecture   an art gallery   a museum   a concert

1 ....*A museum*........ contains objects from history.

2 .... is a musical performance.

3 .... means the design and creation of buildings.

4 .... has collections of paintings and sculptures.

2 Adjectives are used to describe things, experiences and people. Some adjectives are positive and some are negative.

*The exhibition at the gallery was **boring**.* (= negative)
*Adele is a **fantastic** singer.* (= positive)

Decide if the adjectives below are positive (P) or negative (N). Write P or N next to each one.

useful	dangerous N	interesting	tiring	creative
amazing	beautiful	harmless		terrible

Now complete the texts below with the adjectives above. (More than one answer may be possible.)

A: We went to the opera last weekend and I enjoyed it very much. The singers were **(1)** _amazing_ and the costumes were **(2)** _____ – all decorated with gold and jewels. The only bad part was that the performance was very long, three hours in total, so it was **(3)** _____. I fell asleep as soon as we arrived home!

B: I definitely recommend the dinosaur exhibition at the Natural History Museum. It is really **(1)** _____ because it explains everything clearly. The exhibition has two sections: one is about the **(2)** _____ dinosaurs that ate other dinosaurs, and the other section is about the **(3)** _____ dinosaurs that just ate plants. The only bad thing about the exhibition is that some of the dinosaur drawings are **(4)** _____. They don't look like dinosaurs at all!

3 The word order of a simple statement in English is: Subject + Verb + Object. Extra information usually comes after this structure.

Subject + <u>Verb</u> + *Object* + extra information
Picasso <u>*painted*</u> *the picture* at his studio in Paris.

Put the words and phrases in the correct order to make sentences.

1 a film / on Saturday night / My family / watched
   My family watched a film on Saturday night.

2 a bestselling book / Louise / gave me / for my birthday
   ....

3 saw / a Shakespeare play / My sister and I / in London
   ....

4 has / many interesting art galleries / Tokyo / nowadays
   ....

5 opera / like / Older people / more than young people
   ....

6 on the Internet / music / Most teenagers / listen to
   ....

Watch Out!

English word order is not usually flexible. Don't change the order S + V + O.

~~The film I like very much.~~   *I like the film very much.*

~~I visited with my friend the art gallery.~~   *I visited the art gallery with my friend.*

Unit 4 Places to live

Speaking — Different cities

Vocabulary: Places in cities

A

B

C

1 Match the photos A–C with the places below. There are three extra places.

> football stadium   gallery   harbour
> market   museum   shopping mall

2 Look at the photos again. What can you do in each place? Choose activities from the list.

> buy clothes   go on a boat trip
> have a coffee   see an exhibition

Example: *You can buy clothes in a shopping mall.*

3 Look at the places below. Where can you do activities 1–5? Can you add more places?

> beach   bridge   café   factory
> gallery   hotel   park   river
>   skyscraper   theatre

1 eat or drink something

2 go for a walk

3 relax and meet friends

4 work

5 see a view of the city

Vocabulary: Describing cities

4 Match sentences 1–5 with their meanings a–e.

1 It's a <u>busy</u> city.

2 It's near the <u>beach</u>.

3 It's got <u>different neighbourhoods</u>.

4 It's famous for its <u>markets</u>.

5 I really like it because <u>the people are very friendly</u>.

a I go swimming there at the weekend. Sometimes we go sailing too.

b They're polite and they're very happy when you speak their language.

c There's a lot of traffic and people say the city never sleeps!

d Tourists buy clothes or souvenirs. You can even go on tours.

e There's a financial district, a busy downtown and quiet suburbs.

5 Replace the <u>underlined</u> words and phrases in Exercise 4 to make more sentences about cities. Use the words below or your own ideas.

airport	beautiful	museums	mountains
traditional food	lots of tourist attractions	modern	the weather is good

Example: *It's a modern city.*

6 Complete the sentences so they are true for your hometown.

1 It's a .... city.

2 It's near the ....

3 It's got ....

4 It's famous for its ....

5 I really like it because ....

Pronunciation: Syllables and word stress

14 **7** Look at the words in Exercise 3 again. How many syllables (different word parts) are there? Complete the table. Then listen and check.

One syllable	Two syllables	Three syllables
beach	café	

15 **8** Listen to the words again and underline the syllable that has the word stress.

Grammar: *There is / There are*

16 **9** Listen to Sam describing a city. Write the words below next to the correct phrase.

accommodation	beach	harbours	markets	~~museum~~	people	shopping malls	traffic

There's a .... *museum* ....

There isn't ....

There are ....

There aren't ....

10 Complete the table with the correct words.

+	There	's / is	a museum.	
		(1)	some galleries.	
–	There	(2) .... / is not	a beach.	
		aren't / (3)	any harbours.	
?	Is		a football stadium?	Yes, there is.
		there		(5) .... , there isn't.
	(4)		any shopping malls?	Yes, there (6) ....
				No, there (7) ....

Watch Out!

Countable nouns have two forms:	Uncountable nouns have one form:
There is a museum. (singular)	*There isn't any accommodation.*
There are two museums. (plural)	~~*There aren't any accommodations.*~~

11 Read the text and complete each paragraph with the correct words.

bridge	famous	got	near	skyscrapers

My hometown is (**1**) .... the border. It's a busy city and it's (**2**) ....
for its different neighbourhoods. It's (**3**) .... a financial district with lots of tall
(**4**) .... You can walk over a modern (**5**) .... to the harbour.

are	can	favourite	meet	traditional

My (**6**) .... place is the historic centre. You (**7**) .... go to lots of small
restaurants and eat (**8**) .... food. It's delicious! It's a great place to (**9**) ....
friends. There (**10**) .... always lots of people there. It's a popular place.

Writing

Living in cities: population and amenities

1 Match the words below with the pictures 1–6.

shopping centre	industrial area	~~residential area~~
entertainment complex	sports centre	business park

1 *residential area*

2 ....

3 ....

4 ....

5 ....

6 ....

2 Match the verbs 1–8 with their definitions a–h.

1	to improve	*d*	a	to become larger
2	to expand		b	to change something slightly
3	to alter something		c	to make something smaller
4	to deteriorate		d	to become better

5	to reduce something			e	to increase in size or number
6	to convert something			f	to become worse
7	to transform something			g	to change the form or purpose of something
8	to grow			h	to change something completely

3 **Now choose the correct verb to complete each sentence.**

1 They decided to *convert / grow* the old factory into a shopping centre.

2 The population of London has *improved / expanded* to over eight million.

3 I didn't recognize Tom when I saw him. He has *converted / altered* a lot since university.

4 We want to *improve / deteriorate* the public transport system so more people will use the trains and buses.

5 The new motorway has *reduced / converted* the amount of time it takes to get from London to Oxford.

6 The number of people using the Internet is *growing / improving* all the time.

7 This was a nice town a few years ago, but it has *reduced / deteriorated* a lot.

8 The Internet is *growing / transforming* the way that people shop.

Watch Out!

The present perfect cannot be used to talk about past events in the same way as the past simple. It is usually used to talk about things that happened during a period of time that comes right up to the present and perhaps continues into the future. For example:

The population of London started to expand in the 1990s. (The expansion started at a specific time in the past.)

The population of London has expanded to over 8 million. (The expansion happened over a period of time that began in the 1990s and continues up until now.)

4 **Look at these examples of comparative and superlative forms.**

*The population of Summerville was the **highest** in 2010.*

*The average house price was **higher** in 2010 **than** in 2005.*

Read the information in the table about the town of Summerville and choose the correct words in the sentences below.

Changes in Summerville 2000–2010			
	2000	2005	2010
Average house prices	$150,000	$155,000	$159,000
Population	45,000	53,000	61,000
Number of houses built	240	190	175
Number of sports centres	0	2	2
Number of entertainment complexes	2	2	3

1 Summerville had a *smaller / largest / higher* population in 2005 than 2000.

2 Average house prices were the *lowest / highest / tallest* in 2010.

3 In 2000 the population was the *higher / greatest / lowest*.

4 The number of *houses / sports centres / entertainment complexes* built was higher in 2010 than 2005.

5 The number of houses built in 2000 was *lower / higher / the largest*.

1 The pictures symbolize different aspects of 'community'. Read the definitions in the second column and complete the words in the first column with the words below.

> spirit   centre   college   service   policing   care

1 community	a place that is specially provided for the people, groups and organizations in a particular area, where they can go in order to meet one another and do things
2 community	an educational institution in the USA where students from the surrounding area can take courses in practical or academic subjects
3 community	a system in which the police work only in one particular area of the community, so that everyone knows them. In Britain, there are Community Support Officers, volunteers who are trained to prevent and solve low-level crimes so that people feel safer
4 community	unpaid work that criminals sometimes do as a punishment instead of being sent to prison
5 community	help available to persons living in their own homes, rather than services provided in residential institutions
6 community	the feeling of loyalty to a group that is shared by the people who belong to the group

2 The word *community* contains information about its meaning and its grammatical category: it is similar to the word *common*, and the *-ity* ending tells us that the word is a noun.

What do you think the words in the table below mean? Choose from the options below the table. What grammatical category do they belong to?

	Grammatical category	Meaning
communal		
a commune		
a communist		

a a supporter of communism (the political belief that all people are equal and that workers should control the means of producing things)

b a group of people who live together and share everything

c belonging or relating to a community as a whole; something that is shared

3 Categorize the words in the first column by ticking under the appropriate heading(s). There may be more than one answer. Then complete the other boxes with the appropriate part of speech where possible.

	Adjective	Verb	Adverb	Noun
criminal				
volunteer				
loyalty				
residential				
punish				

4 Match 1–7 with a–g to make two-part words that describe groups of people.

1	political	a	party
2	online	b	cast
3	voluntary	c	band
4	film	d	group
5	rock	e	team
6	friendship	f	community
7	sports	g	organization

Watch Out!

It is important to recognize what the pronouns in a text refer to. Be careful with *they*, *their* and *them*: they do not always relate to plural forms. They are often used to talk about individuals to avoid mentioning gender (*he* or *she*, *his* or *her*, *him* or *her*).

A team member must be prepared to put other people's needs before their own. (avoids the use of 'his/her own')

Campus services

1 .... 2 .... 3 .... 4 ....

1 The pictures above show buildings on a university campus. Label the buildings with the words below.

> halls of residence   library   medical centre   sports centre

2 Now match the buildings in Exercise 1 with the definitions below. You will not use all the definitions.

1 This is where you go to get fit. ....

2 You go here when you are sick and need to get a prescription. ....

3 This is where you will find all kinds of reference materials, including journals, films, computers and all the information you need for your studies. ....

4 This is where students live on campus. ....

Spelling

Watch Out!

Some words sound the same, but are spelt differently. In the Listening test, you must spell your answers correctly or you will lose points.

3 Choose the correct spelling to complete the sentences.

1 The lecturer told his students to read .... the article quickly.
(*threw / through / though*)

2 .... was a long queue of people waiting at the medical centre to see the doctor.
(*Their / They're / There*)

3 The university has a number of .... (*restuarants / restaurants / restaurents*)

4 A lot of people enjoy meeting visitors from .... countries. (*foriegn / foreing / foreign*)

5 To get to the library, take the first road on the left and keep walking .... you get to the end of the road. (*untill / until / unntil*)

6 The tutor's office is on the .... floor. (*twelvth / twefth / twelfth*).

Prepositions

4 Sometimes there is more than one word to describe the same position, for example: *beside, by, next to*. In each group of words, circle the preposition or phrase that does NOT belong to the group.

1 on top of, into, over, above

2 next to, far away, nearby, close to

3 outside, inside, within, into

4 behind, opposite, in front of, facing

5 beside, next to, between, at the side of

5 Read the description of a university campus and label the buildings on the plan.

The library is in the middle of the campus. It's next to the theatre. There's a shop behind the library, between the bank and the bookshop. The Student Union building is opposite the theatre, beside the round building, which is the night club. The sports centre is on the other side of the green, facing the medical centre.

A Sports Centre   **B** Night Club   **C** Student Union   **D** Shop   **E** Theatre

Bookshop	(2)	Bank

(3)	(1)	Library	Green	(5) .....
(4)				

Canteen		Medical Centre

Unit **5** Arts and media

Writing — Films

1 **Read the definitions below and complete the types of film.**

1 A film that makes people laugh. c <u>o</u> <u>m</u> <u>e</u> <u>d</u> y

2 This type of film has a hero as the main character. a _ _ _ _ _

3 A factual programme about an event or a person. d _ _ _ _ _ _ _ _ _ _

4 A crime or mystery film which is exciting. t _ _ _ _ _ _ _

5 A film which makes people afraid. h _ _ _ _ _ f _ _ _

6 A film based on space and the future. s _ _ _ _ _ _ f _ _ _

2 **Circle the correct option.**

In Hollywood famous actors often play the main (**1**) *character / personality* in a film. The films usually have music or a (**2**) *CD / soundtrack* to increase the atmosphere. Hollywood films often have a simple (**3**) *history / story* and use special (**4**) *effects / factors* such as explosions to make the film exciting. Hollywood films can be divided into different (**5**) *genres / topics,* such as thrillers or romantic films. If films are very successful, they are called (**6**) *movies / blockbusters.*

3 **Complete the film descriptions using words from Exercises 1 and 2.**

1 This film is a .... that tells the true .... of a woman who lived in Russia in the twentieth century and became a famous film director.

2 *Blackout* is a .... film set in the twenty-second century. It follows a group of explorers as they visit other planets and try to stay alive. There are lots of ...., such as giant spaceships and explosions.

3 The .... of film that is most popular with teenage girls is romantic comedy. They also like film music and buy more CDs of film .... than boys. However, in general girls find .... films too frightening.

4 **Percentages (%) and fractions (¼, ⅓ , ½, etc.) can both be used to describe proportions of a whole amount.**

a half	a quarter	three quarters	a third	two thirds

Match the percentages with the fractions.

50 per cent	25 per cent	75 per cent	33 per cent	66 per cent
two thirds	a half	a third	a quarter	three quarters

Watch Out!

Per cent is used with a number, e.g. *ten per cent, 50 per cent.*

Percentage is used with words, e.g. *the percentage of people, a small percentage of people.*

5 **Use these patterns to write about percentages and fractions:**

fraction + *of* + noun + verb   *per cent* + *of* + noun + verb

A quarter of the people like horror films.   *Twenty per cent of teenagers don't like action films.*

Teenagers spent a third of the time watching   *Ten per cent of boys like action films.*
documentaries.

Put the words in the correct order to make sentences.

1 of adults / science fiction / watch / a third / films / do not

....

2 Bollywood / of worldwide film sales / ten per cent / come from

....

3 three quarters of / films / on television / people over 65 / watch

....

4 cartoons / children / on a regular basis / ninety per cent of / watch

....

6 **If you do not know precise numbers or quantities, you can use words and phrases that express approximate amounts. Look at the bold words in these examples.**

About / Approximately *a third of UK film sales in 2009 were comedy films.*

Just under / Almost / Nearly a third of *UK film sales in 2009 were thrillers.*

Now match the percentages 1–4 with the phrases a–d.

1 53 per cent   a just under a quarter

2 30 per cent   b almost all

3 95 per cent   c approximately half

4 23 per cent   d about a third

Reading   Books

1   2   3   4   5   6

1   **Match the words with the books 1–6.**

| a comic | a dictionary | a guide | a journal | a biography | a mystery |

1 ....   4 ....

2 ....   5 ....

3 ....   6 ....

2   **Circle the correct option.**

1 A comic book is a book or newspaper that has a series of *paragraphs / drawings* that tell a humorous story or an adventure.

2 A journal is often personal because it is a record of someone's *secrets / daily activities*.

3 A trilogy is a group of three books with *the same subject or characters / a different subject or different characters*.

4 A biography tells the story of someone's life and is written by *that person / another person*.

5 A travel guide is a *book / newspaper* that gives tourists information about a town, area or country.

3   **Put the words from Exercise 1 in the correct column.**

Fiction: books and stories that are not about real people or events	**Non-fiction:** writing that gives information or describes real events

4   **Word parts can give important information about meaning. Read the information in the table. Then complete the matching exercise below.**

Word part	Meaning
auto-	self; same; of or by the same one
bio-	connected with human life
biblio-	connected with books
dia-	across, between
-graphy	a form of writing or drawing
-logue	speech
mono-	single, one

1 bibliography	**a**	a conversation between two people in a book or play
2 autobiography	**b**	an account of your life, which you write yourself
3 monologue	**c**	a long speech spoken by one person, often as entertainment such as part of a play
4 dialogue	**d**	a list of books that have been written about a particular subject or that have been mentioned in a book or an article

5 **Complete the book review below with words from Exercises 1 and 3.**

One of the classics of English literature is *Jane Eyre*. Although the title is the name of a woman, the book is a work of fiction, not a **(1)** .... or **(2)** .... The book was published in 1847. It tells the story of the heroine, Jane Eyre. Jane has a difficult childhood but she finds happiness when she is older. She goes to work for a man called Edward Rochester and they fall in love. However, he has a secret which will separate him and Jane. My favourite parts of the book are those between Jane and Mr Rochester as there are some funny **(3)** .... between them. I also like that the fact that the book is not just a romantic story: there are many things the reader does not know so it is also a **(4)** .... Most of all, I like the fact that it has a happy ending.

Watch Out!

Knowing the meaning of word parts can often help you work out the overall meaning, but there are words where this does not work. For example, *dis-* often means 'opposite', e.g. *advantage / disadvantage*; *agree / disagree*; *appear / disappear*; *connect / disconnect*; *honest / dishonest*, but sometimes *dis-* is not a separate word part or does not have that meaning, as in *disaster, discuss*.

Speaking TV and radio programmes

Vocabulary: Types of programme

 **A**  **B**  **C**  **D**

1 **Read descriptions 1–6 of different types of programme. Match them with photos A–D. There are two extra descriptions.**

1 I love watching documentaries because we can learn about new things. My favourite is a <u>series</u> about nature and animals.

2 I watch a game show every weekend with my family. I think the <u>presenter</u> is very funny. I like it when the contestants win big prizes.

3 I always listen to the news. I think it's important to understand the events in your country and listen to business reports. You can find out about your sports team too.

4 I enjoy watching soap operas because they are similar to real life and I like the <u>characters</u>. I usually watch TV on my laptop in my room.

5 I sometimes watch talk shows. The <u>guests</u> are really interesting. You can learn about their lives and new films or new music.

6 I'm a sports fan, so I watch a lot of sport on TV. I enjoy listening to the experts talking about the results too.

2 Check the meaning of the underlined words in Exercise 1. Then answer the questions.

1 Do you have a favourite TV presenter? Why do you like him/her?

2 What is a popular documentary series in your country?

3 Are there any characters in a soap opera you really like?

4 Do you think most guests on a talk show are interesting?

Vocabulary: Describing programmes

3 Listen to three people talking about programmes they listen to or watch. Match the speakers, 1–3, with the type of programme they watch, a–c.

a documentary series ....

b drama series ....

c reality TV show ....

4 Read sentences a–h. Listen again and decide which speaker, 1–3, says each sentence. Which three sentences express an opinion?

a It's about clothes and the fashion industry. ....

b It's set in London. ....

c It's presented by different models each week. ....

d It stars some famous actors. ....

e The participants are famous people. ....

f It's very exciting. ....

g I think it's good entertainment. ....

h The thing I like best is the hotel manager. ....

5 Think about a programme you enjoy watching or listening to. Write sentences to describe it and express your opinion about it. Use the sentences in Exercise 4 to help you.

Watch Out!

actors = people who play characters in a story

characters = people in a story

contestants = real people in a game show or reality TV show

Grammar: Adverbs of frequency

6 Match sentences 1–6 with explanations a–f. Which sentences are true for you?

1 I always watch soap operas.

2 I usually listen to the news in the morning.

3 I often watch game shows.

4 I sometimes watch dramas.

5 I rarely listen to sports programmes.

6 I never watch documentaries.

a I'm not interested in any sports.

b I think they're very boring.

c I like it when contestants win big prizes.

d I think the plots are sometimes interesting.

e I watch them every day. I never miss an episode.

f I like listening to the business reports.

7 Look at the arrow and the adverbs of frequency. Put the words *always*, *often* and *rarely* in the correct position on the arrow.

never   (1) ....   sometimes   (2) ....   usually   (3) ....

Watch Out!

The adverb of frequency goes <u>before</u> the verb: *I always watch films*.

BUT it goes <u>after</u> the verb **to be**: *I think the plots are sometimes crazy*.

---

8 Complete the texts with the words below.

1
| by | contestants | every | favourite |

My .... programme is a quiz show called *In, Out*. I watch it .... weekend.
The .... are very clever. It's presented .... a university professor.

2
| about | actors | interesting | operas |

I enjoy watching documentaries .... science. They are very .... I rarely
watch soap .... because I think the .... are terrible.

3
| always | exciting | series | stars |

I like watching a drama .... called *School Time*. I .... watch it with my
brother. It .... our favourite actor and it's a very .... programme.

4
| contestants | funny | sometimes | talk |

I like .... shows. The guests are usually very .... I like game shows too.
The .... on game shows are .... really good.

Listening   Communicating information

1 You can find these words about crime and staying safe in newspapers and magazines. Tick the ones you can see in the pictures.

break into ☐   thief ☐   knife ☐   gun ☐   gang ☐   pickpocket ☐

2 Write the words in correct columns in the table.

crime	knife	gun	gang	dangerous	careful
steal	rob	break into	thief	attack	safe

Noun	Verb	Adjective

Words with similar meanings

Watch Out!

If you don't read questions carefully before you do a listening activity, you won't notice the key words. You should not only notice them but also think about possible synonyms. This will help you to predict what you will hear.

3 The following information comes from a university magazine under the section: *Watch Out! There are thieves about!* Complete the sentences with the words below that have the same meaning as the word in brackets. Make sure your answers are grammatically correct.

| steal | safe | robber | shoplifter | gang | pickpocket | burglar |

1 Last week, a (thief) broke into the student union office and (took) a laptop.

2 While the friends were in the university sports hall, a (thief) took their wallets out of their jackets.

3 A police officer went to the campus bookshop to talk to a (thief) who was taking books out of the shop without paying.

4 A (group) of (thieves) broke into the campus bank over the weekend and took thousands of pounds.

5 Students are advised to keep their belongings in a (secure) place when they are using the university's sports facilities.

Collocations

Some words are often used together. For example: *do + homework*, *make + cake*. In the exam, it will help to know which words go together and what you expect to hear.

4 Match the words 1–5 with the words a–e that are often used together.

1	take	a	the police
2	watch out	b	up
3	call	c	for
4	lock	d	scene
5	crime	e	to court

5 **Complete the newspaper extract with phrases from Exercise 4. Check that the verb tenses are correct.**

When the receptionist arrived at Goodmead Primary School on Monday, she found that someone had broken into the office and stolen several laptops, so she (**1**) .... They came to look at the (**2**) .... straight away and advised her to make sure she (**3**) .... the office every evening in future. They also suggested that she should (**4**) .... any strangers nearby. Two days later, the police called to say that they had caught the thieves and arrested them. They said they would (**5**) .... (them) in the next few days.

 6 **Listen to the recording and check your answers.**

Pronunciation

When you listen to people speaking, it is sometimes difficult to hear the end of one word and the beginning of the next. This often happens when:

- the first word ends with the same sound that starts the next word, e.g. *take care*.
- the second word begins with a vowel e.g. *watch out*.

 7 **Listen to this sentence from the recording and underline where the words join together.**

When the receptionist arrived at Goodmead Primary school on Monday, she found that someone had broken into the office and stolen several laptops, so she called the police.

Unit 6 The natural world

Weather

Vocabulary: The weather

A

B

C

D

1 Match two words with each picture A–D above.

> cold   hot   rainy   snowy   stormy   sunny   wet   windy

2 Use your answers from Exercise 1 to complete the descriptions below.

Picture A   In my country, the monsoon season is from September to November.
It's very .... and ....

Picture B   In my country, winter lasts from December to February.
It's .... and ....

Picture C   We often have thunderstorms in March or April in my country.
It's .... and ....

Picture D   The dry season lasts from May until October in my country.
It's .... and ....

3 Complete the table below with information about the seasons in your country.

Season	Months	Weather
autumn	October and November	cold and windy
dry season		
rainy season		
spring		
summer		
winter		

Vocabulary: Talking about the weather

4 **Complete the sentences with the words and phrases below.**

favourite	it's	lasts	makes	really like	there's

1 My _____ season is summer.

2 _____ lots of rain during the monsoon season.

3 In winter, _____ wet and stormy in my country.

4 Hot weather _____ me feel really happy.

5 Winter _____ for two months.

6 I _____ stormy weather because it's exciting.

> **Watch Out!**
>
> **It's + adjective** = *It's rainy / snowy / windy.*
>
> **There's / There are + noun** = *There's lots of rain / snow / wind.*

5 **Complete the sentences with your own ideas.**

1 My favourites season is _____.

2 In summer, it's _____.

3 There's lots of rain / sun during _____.

4 Summer / The dry season lasts for _____.

5 Cold weather makes me feel _____.

6 I really like _____.

Pronunciation: Vowel sounds

20 **6** **Listen to the vowel sounds and the words, and repeat them.**

/uː/	/aʊ/	/ʌ/	/eɪ/	/ɔː/	/əʊ/
monsoon	now	summer	favourite	stormy	cold

21 **7** **Listen to the words below and add them to the correct vowel sound in the table in Exercise 6. Use a dictionary to check the meaning of the words.**

April	autumn	drought	humid	June	month
November	outside	rainy	snowy	stormy	sunny

22 **8** **Listen and check. Then listen again and repeat the vowel sounds and the words.**

Grammar: *Can / can't*

23 **9** **Listen and complete the sentences with *can* or *can't*.**

1 You _____ go to the beach in the summer.

2 You _____ do anything when the weather is very hot.

3 You _____ play tennis outside when it's rainy.

4 The rainy season _____ last for weeks.

5 You _____ go skiing in hot and dry climates.

6 The weather _____ change quickly in the mountains.

10 Read the rules about *can* and *can't*. Then complete the sentences with your own ideas.

- We use *can* to say that it is possible to do something.
- We use *can't* to say that it is not possible to do something.
- Put *can* or *can't* before the main verb.
- The form of the main verb doesn't change.

1 When it's sunny, you can ....

2 In cold weather, you can't ....

3 In summer, you can ....

4 In the rainy season, you can't ....

11 Complete the sentences with the words below. There is one extra word in each set.

1

can	it's	makes	season	weather

My favourite .... is summer. I really like the summer because .... always hot and sunny. You .... do lots of sports or you can sunbathe and relax with friends. The hot weather always .... me feel happy and cheerful. I think everybody likes the hot weather.

2

can't	drought	dry	for	monsoon

A .... means lots of rainy weather! In my country, this season lasts .... about three or four months. It's boring and you .... do anything outside. It's humid and I don't like it. I prefer the .... weather because I like being outside.

3

can	from	stormy	there's	thunderstorms

In my country, it's very cold in winter. .... lots of snow and you .... go skiing or visit the mountains. This is my favourite season. It lasts .... November to February. It's different from summer because summer lasts for about six months. It's really hot and dry and there are .... at night.

Listening

The oceans as a natural resource

1

2

3

4

1 Each picture shows a different way of using the ocean. Copy and complete the table with the words and phrases below. Some can go into more than one column.

oil rig	natural gas	trawler	mineral resource	off-shore drilling	fish farm
underwater turbine		wave power	gas pipeline	energy	fuel	net

Picture 1	Picture 2	Picture 3	Picture 4
oil rig			

2 **Match the phrases 1–6 with the definitions a–f.**

1 off-shore drilling

2 mineral

3 fuel

4 trawler

5 rig

a a large structure for drilling for oil from the sea bed

b a material that is burned to produce power

c a type of fishing boat

d a natural material

e a method of extracting oil from the sea bed

3 **Find and correct the mistake in each sentence.**

1 Oil is a non-renewable sauce of energy.

2 Trawlers sometimes spend many months at see.

3 Off-shore drilling has effected wildlife in this area.

4 We need fuel for are car.

5 Underwater turbines capture energy from ocean currants.

Trends and statistics

Statistics are the numbers which record facts (like the number of births and deaths in a year) and the words that describe these numbers in relation to the whole group.

113 fishing boats were lost at sea last year.

20% of the fish population is currently at risk of disappearing.

*The **majority** of our electricity could be generated by wave power.*

Trends describe *patterns of change* in social behaviour or environmental conditions over a period of time and may tell us how much they have changed.

*Since 2009, interest in wave power has **increased significantly**.*

*There has been a **dramatic rise** in fish farming **over the last ten years**.*

***During this century** there has been an **upward trend** in global temperatures.*

4 **Look at the graphs below. Do they show trends or statistics? Match the statements with the graphs.**

1 The number of destructive storms has increased significantly in the last ten years.

2 There has been a gradual rise in temperature across the globe recently.

3 The polar bear population has fallen dramatically since 2010.

4 The frequency of volcanic eruptions has remained stable over the past century.

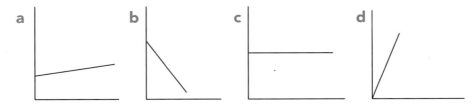

5 The words below are used to describe *statistics* and *trends*. Copy and complete the table, and say whether they are nouns, verbs, adjectives or adverbs. The first one has been done for you.

rise	average	gradual	per cent	more than	fall	majority
increase	decrease	minority	remain stable	less than	downward	fraction
upward	number	slight	tendency	amount	significant	dramatic

Statistics	Trends
....	*rise* (noun/verb)

Writing   Natural and unnatural processes

1 Match the words 1–10 with their definitions a–j.

1	volcano	e	a	a building where things are made using machines
2	acid rain	☐	b	damage caused to nature by chemicals or waste
3	glacier	☐	c	the mixture of gases around the Earth
4	factory	☐	d	the measurement of heat or cold
5	to harvest	☐	e	a mountain with a hole at the top where lava comes out
6	pollution	☐	f	to explode
7	to erupt	☐	g	a large river of ice which moves slowly
8	atmosphere	☐	h	a form of energy that comes from a nuclear reaction
9	temperature	☐	i	rain which contains large amounts of harmful chemicals
10	radiation	☐	j	to pick and collect crops or plants

2 Now complete the sentences with the correct form of the words from Exercise 1.

1 In summer it can be very hot here; the .... can reach 40°C.

2 The plants were destroyed by .... from the factory.

3 Farmers .... their crops at the end of summer.

4 The volcano .... and lava started to flow down the mountain.

3 Number the phrases below 1–6 to describe the stages in a plant's life.

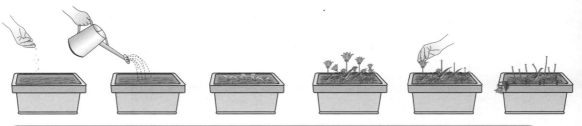

plants grow	flowers are picked	seeds are watered
seeds are planted *1*	plants die	plants flower

4 **We can use the passive to describe a process. We use the passive:**

1 when who or what did the action (= the agent) is not known.

2 when who or what did the action is not important.

3 when we want to focus on the object of the action more than the subject.

Passive: *Volcanoes **are formed** by the movement of the Earth's surface.*
Active: *The movement of the Earth's surface **forms** volcanoes.*

Passive: *Bananas **are grown** in hot climates.*
Active: *People **grow** bananas in hot climates.*

We form the passive with the verb *to be* + past participle. Sometimes an agent with *by* is included.
*Seeds are planted **by farmers**.*

Sometimes there is no agent.
Seeds are planted in the fields.

Complete the sentences using present simple passive forms of the verbs in brackets.

1 Water ....*is stored*............ (store) in reservoirs and used in the fields.

2 Grass .... (eat) by cows and cows .... (eat) by people.

3 Many buildings .... (destroy) by bad storms in winter.

4 Rainforests .... (inhabit) by thousands of plants and insects.

5 Forests .... (damage) by acid rain.

6 Most pollution .... (cause) by human activity.

5 **Correct the errors in the passive in these sentences.**

1 In many countries birds ~~is~~ *are* fed by people in the winter.

2 Chemicals are used farmers to protect plants from insects.

3 Seeds are plant in the spring.

4 Elephants and camels used as working animals in some countries.

5 Volcanic eruptions and other natural disasters is studied by scientists.

6 Fields be watered by a special system called irrigation.

Watch Out!

Remember that the present simple passive of ordinary verbs must have a form of the verb
to be (not the infinitive without *to: be*).

~~Gazelles be hunted by tigers~~.	*Gazelles **are** hunted by tigers.*
~~Wildlife to be protected by laws~~.	*Wildlife **is** protected by laws.*

1 .... 2 .... 3 .... 4 ....

1 **The following words refer to the natural world. Use the words to label the pictures above.**

> bay   valley   cliff   waterfall

2 **The words below refer to similar things, but they are not interchangeable. Choose the correct words to complete the sentences.**

> soil   sand   land   ground

1 The house we are buying comes with a lot of ....

2 Children love playing in the ....

3 There were no chairs in the garden so we all sat on the ....

4 I have bought a big bag of .... so I can plant some flowers in these pots.

3 **Read the texts below without using a dictionary. Underline the words that refer to the natural world, and circle all the linking words.**

Our knowledge of Natural History would not be what it is today without the work of women explorers, artists and scientists. In this leaflet, you will learn about three British pioneering women, among the first to be involved in uncovering some of the rich history of the natural world.

Mary Anning (1799–1847)

Mary came from a poor family who lived in Lyme Regis, a town on the south-west coast of England. Her father tried to make extra money by selling fossils (plant and animal remains in rocks) to rich tourists. Consequently, Mary and her siblings learnt from an early age how to look for fossils, although she was the only one of the brothers and sisters who became an expert.

However, in her lifetime she did not always get the credit she deserved, as it was male geologists who published the descriptions of any finds. Her important finds include the first skeleton of an ichthyosaur, or fish-lizard, a plesiosaur, also known as sea-dragon, and a pterodactyl, or a 'flying dragon'.

Collecting fossils on the cliffs was dangerous work. Mary's dog Tray was killed when rocks and earth fell down a cliff, and she nearly lost her life in the same landslide.

Dorothea Bate (1878–1951)

Born in the Welsh countryside, she had a passion for outdoor pursuits and natural history from an early age. She became the first female scientist in the Natural History Museum in London. She was a palaeontologist, that is, a scientist who studies fossils in order to understand the history of life on Earth. She went to mountains and cliffs in the Mediterranean and explored hilltops in Bethlehem, discovering and documenting animal fossils. She wrote hundreds of reports, reviews and papers.

Evelyn Cheesman (1881–1969)

Although Evelyn wanted to become a veterinary surgeon, this was not possible for women in the early twentieth century. Instead, she trained as a canine nurse. Her first job, however, was not related to dogs: she worked in the insect house at the London Zoological Society. She was very adventurous and went on many expeditions to remote locations, as far away as the Galapagos Islands. Despite being very busy, she managed to publish 16 books.

4 **Difficult words are often explained in texts. Find the explanations of the words below in the texts in Exercise 3. The first one has been done for you.**

| pioneering | Lyme Regis | fossils | siblings | ichthyosaur | plesiosaur |
| pterodactyl | Tray | landslide | palaeontologist | canine | remote |

pioneering — (among) the first

Watch Out!

The exact meaning of linking words is not always clear. For example, 'in fact' is not used just to introduce <u>any</u> facts; they have to be <u>surprising</u> or <u>contrasting</u> facts, in comparison to what has just been said.

✗ *Many people argue as to who is more intelligent, women or men. In fact, a study found that women scientists are more intelligent than men in similar jobs.*

✓ *In the past, people thought that women were less intelligent than men because of genetic differences. In fact, according to one study, women scientists are more intelligent than men in similar jobs.*

5 **Do the following extracts use *in fact* correctly? Mark each extract with a ✓ or ✗.**

1 It is often believed that watching a lot of TV makes people see the world as a frightening place. In fact, evidence shows that watching TV makes no difference.

2 It is often believed that watching a lot of TV makes people see the world as a frightening place. In fact, there is some evidence that this is the case.

Unit **7** Education

Writing

School, college and university

1 **Look at the pictures. Complete the sentences by putting the letters of the bold words in the correct order.**

1 At school, you have **s a l c s e s** .... for different subjects, such as maths, science and history.

2 The **e t r e a h c** .... will answer any questions you may have.

3 Sometimes at the end of the year, students take an **m e a x** .... to check what they have learnt.

4 Some students go on to university, where they will learn through seminars and **c t u r s e l e** ....

5 Sometimes a university student gives a **s e i n r t a p n e t o** .... to other students.

2 **Unscramble the verbs in the box, and then put each one next to a noun in the table to make a collocation. (You can use each verb more than once, and each noun can have more than one verb.)**

| ktea | its | od | vegi | wetir | duyts | kema | spas | ifla | teg |

Verbs	Nouns	Verbs	Nouns
take	an exam		an essay
	a qualification		a subject (e.g. biology)
	a course		a presentation

Watch Out!

To pass an exam means to reach the required grade or pass mark, not to take the exam.

Complete the text with verbs from the table.

Mustafa: I've just finished school. I **(1)** .... all my exams, so I'm really happy! I'm going to go to university. I want to **(2)** .... engineering. I have to **(3)** ....
an entrance exam for my English because I want to study in Australia. The course sounds really good.
It's at a really good university and has a mixture of assessments; I'll need to **(4)** .... essays,
(5) .... presentations and **(6)** .... exams. I'll also get some work
experience! It's a lot of work but I think I'll **(7)** .... a really good qualification.

3 Now look at the verb + noun collocations in the sentences below. Circle the correct verbs. If necessary, use your dictionary to check.

1 Amil *took / gave* an online test to find out how good his grammar was.

2 When the course finished, all of the students had to complete a feedback form and *make / give* our opinions about the university and the teaching staff.

3 Our students *take / have* lectures in the mornings and self-study in the afternoons.

4 At the end of the course you *get / give* a certificate of attendance.

5 Did you *make / do* your maths homework?

6 It's a good idea to *get / take* some work experience while you are at university. It could help you find a job later.

7 I have two assignments to *make / do* before Friday.

8 Can you *take / give* us examples of the essay questions we might have to answer?

4 The notes show what the class of 2013 did after they left school. Read the notes and complete the sentences with the correct information and the correct form of the verbs in brackets.

> Destinations of school leavers, 2013
> University: 12 boys 14 girls
> Local college: 7 boys 1 girl
> Work: 5 boys 8 girls

1 .... girls .... (go) to university after leaving school.

2 .... girl .... (start) courses at the local further education college.

3 .... boys and .... girls .... (find) jobs straight after leaving high school.

4 .... school leavers .... (continue) studying after leaving school.

5 Only .... school leavers .... (not go) to university or college.

6 .... school leavers .... (decide) to go to college.

5 We can also use comparative forms to compare information. Look at the information in the notes below and choose the best way to complete the grammar notes.

> Student numbers at local primary schools, 2014
> Percival School: 80 boys, 40 girls
> St James School: 100 boys, 100 girls
> Roysters School: 60 boys, 80 girls
> Bilsing School: 35 boys, 35 girls

- *As much / many* + noun + *as* (to show a quantity is ....): *St James School had as many boys as girls in 2014.*

- *Not as much / many* + noun + *as* + noun (to show that a quantity is .... / **more**): *Percival School didn't have as many girls as St James School.*

- *More* + noun + *than* + noun (to show one quantity is **smaller** / .... than another): *Percival School had more boys than girls.*

- *Less / fewer* + noun + *than* + noun (to show one quantity is .... / **bigger** than another): *Percival School had fewer boys than St James School* (Note: .... / .... is used for countable nouns, and .... / **less** for uncountable nouns.)

Now complete the sentences about Roysters and Bilsing schools using the words in brackets.

1 Roysters School had .... (girls / boys) in 2014.

2 Bilsing School had .... (boys / girls).

3 Roysters School had .... (boys / girls)

4 Bilsing School had (students) .... Roysters School.

5 Roysters School had (students) .... Bilsing School.

Speaking   University study

Vocabulary: Academic subjects

 **A**    **B**    **C**   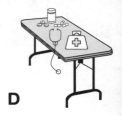 **D**

1 | Match four of the subjects below to the pictures above. Use your dictionary to help you.

> art   business studies   computer science   engineering   history
> law   linguistics   literature   mathematics   medicine

24 2 | Listen to three students talking about their course. Complete each description with the words below. Then listen again and check.

> course   difficult   director   doctor   interesting   law   lawyer   lectures   medicine

1 I'm studying .... It's hard work and there are lots of ...., but I enjoy helping people. I'm in my first year and I'd like to be a ....

2 I'm doing a business studies .... This semester I'm learning about finance and marketing. It's really .... I'd like to be a company ....

3 I'm studying ...., so I'm learning about the legal system. It's a very .... course and there are lots of deadlines. I'd like to be a ....

Watch Out!

I'm **studying** medicine.   I'm **learning about** health and illness.

Pronunciation: Word stress

3 | How many syllables are in these words?

business ....   mathematics ....

literature ....   university ....

25 4 | Listen and check. Then listen again and add the words to the correct stress patterns in the table below.

1 [O o]	2 [O o o]	3 [o o O o]	4 [o o O o o]

26 5 | Listen to the words below and add them to the table in Exercise 4.

> chemistry   college   deadline   engineering   graduate   graduation
> history   lecture   medicine   presentation   project   timetable

27 6 | Listen and check your answers to Exercises 4 and 5. Listen again and repeat the words.

Vocabulary: Collocations

7 Match the verbs 1–5 with the nouns a–e to make collocations about studying. Then match the verbs 6–10 with the nouns f–j to make more collocations.

1	apply	a	presentations	6	go	f	in halls / with my family
2	be	b	for a scholarship	7	graduate	g	extra tuition
3	do	c	good results	8	have	h	to lectures / college
4	get	d	my homework	9	live	i	an essay
5	give	e	in my first / second / final year	10	write	j	from university

8 Complete the sentences with nouns from Exercise 7.

1 I hope I get good .... this semester.

2 I graduated from .... last summer.

3 I'm in my final .... at university.

4 I don't like giving ....

5 I'm writing an .... on international finance.

Grammar: Present continuous

28 **9** Listen to the three speakers. Complete the sentences with the correct names, Lara, Dee or Marcel.

a .... is filling out an application form.

b .... is having extra tuition.

c .... is preparing a presentation.

10 Look at the table and circle the correct word to complete the rule.

- Use the present continuous to talk about an activity happening *in the past / now*.

I	'm	'm not	
He / She / It	's	's not	studying English this semester.
You / We / They	're	're not	

28 **11** Listen to the speakers again and read the texts below. Underline the twelve examples of the present continuous.

1 I'm revising for an exam. It's my final year and I'm working very hard. I'm having extra tuition and my grades are improving.

2 I'm visiting my brother at college. He's living in halls this year and he's having a great time. I'm helping him with his coursework this semester, and we're preparing a presentation at the moment.

3 I'm thinking about doing another course next year. I'm applying for a scholarship at a university in my hometown and I'm filling out the application form now.

12 Complete the sentences below to describe what you are doing.

1 At the moment, I'm ....

2 This semester I'm ....

Watch Out!

at the moment = now or at this time

1 **Match the school subjects 1–4 with the definitions a–d.**

1 numeracy		**a**	a lesson in which pupils do physical exercise or sport
2 literacy		**b**	a school subject in which children learn about religion and other social matters
3 PE		**c**	the ability to work with numbers and do calculations (+, –, x, ÷)
4 RE		**d**	the ability to read and write

2 **Write the correct school subject below each picture, using the words from Exercise 1.**

1 .... 2 .... 3 .... 4 ....

3 **Write down the subjects you studied or are studying at school and write a short definition for each one. Then compare your definitions with those in a dictionary.**

4 **Put the following in order, according to level of education. Rank them from low to high.**

6th form college	nursery school	infant school	master's degree
PhD	secondary school	bachelor's degree	primary school

8 ....

7 ....

6 ....

5 ....

4 ....

3 ....

2 ....

1 ....

5 What do you know about these student destinations and places of origin? Complete the table with the words below.

Arab   Arabic   Brussels   Dutch (x2)   German (x2)   Hanoi   Heidelberg
Japan   Jeddah   Kyoto   Maastricht   Vietnam   Zurich

Country	Main languages	Adjective	City with one or more universities
(1)	Vietnamese	Vietnamese	(2) .... Ho Chi Minh City
(3)	Japanese	Japanese	Tokyo (4) ....
Saudi Arabia	(5)	(6)	Riyadh (7) ....
Germany	(8)	German	(9) .... Munich
The Netherlands	(10)	Dutch	Amsterdam (11) ....
Belgium	(12) .... French	Belgian	Louvain (13) ....
Switzerland	French, Italian (14)	Swiss	Geneva (15) ....

Watch Out!

Remember has two main uses:
(1) to recall people or events from the past, e.g. *I remember how she looked that day.*
(2) to retain an idea or intention in your mind, e.g. *He didn't remember to call me.*
If you help someone else to remember something, you *remind* them about it.
~~Can you remember me to take a coat?~~   *Can you remind me to take a coat?*

6 Complete the sentences with *remember* or *remind*.

1 I will always .... my first day at university.
2 Do you .... which exercises the teacher told us to do?
3 I'll have to .... my friend how to use the slide projector for the presentation.
4 Do you always .... to hand your assignments in on time?
5 Could you .... me to take those books back to the library?

1 **Label the photos with the words below.**

> revision   exam hall   test   text books

1 ....   2 ....   3 ....   4 ....

Comparatives

Look at these examples of comparative sentences:

The population of China is large. It is larger than the population of Italy.
Many students think physics is difficult. They say it is more difficult than art.
Spelling in Spanish is simple. At least, it is simpler than in English.
Some people think playing football is easy. They think it is easier than learning maths.
Exercising in the gym is good for your health, but it is even better to exercise in the fresh air.

Do you know all the different rules (A–E) to form a comparative? Study the table.

A Adjectives with one syllable	B Adjectives with two or three syllables	C Adjectives with two syllables and ending in '-le', '-er', '-ow'	D Adjectives with two syllables and ending in 'y'	E Irregular adjectives
add 'r' or 'er'	put 'more' in front of the adjective	add 'er'	add 'er' and change 'y' to 'i'	change spelling / into another word
large/larger strong/stronger	difficult/more difficult boring/more boring	simple/simpler	easy/easier	far/further

2 **Form the comparative of these adjectives and write them in the correct column in the table below.**

1 fast	3 clever	5 well	7 late	9 bad
2 interesting	4 nervous	6 slow	8 healthy	10 good

+ 'r'	+ 'er'	y + 'ier'	'more' + adjective	irregular adjectives
	faster			

3 Now match your answers with the rules (A–E) in the table on page 54. The first one has been done for you.

1 fast ___A___

2 interesting _____

3 clever _____

4 nervous _____

5 slow _____

6 late _____

7 healthy _____

8 bad _____

9 good _____

4 Complete the paragraph with words from the table in Exercise 2. Use each word once.

Some students think it is (**1**) _____ to study for exams at night, when it is quiet. Others think it is (**2**) _____ to go to bed early and get up early to do their exam revision. A lot of students enjoy studying (**3**) _____ subjects. Some like to revise at the last minute, but (**4**) _____ students need to plan their revision a long time in advance. Students who are (**5**) _____ than average before exams can go to classes to learn relaxation techniques.

Adjectives and adverbs

Watch Out!

Be careful not to confuse adjectives with adverbs.

Adjectives tell us more about nouns. They come before the noun.

Amira is a confident speaker.

Adverbs tell us more about verbs. They usually come after the verb.

Amira spoke confidently about her project on cultural exchanges.

Adverbs can also tell us more about adjectives.

Amira is an exceptionally confident speaker.

5 Choose the words to complete these sentences.

1 The *(intelligently / intelligent)* students answered the exam questions *(correct / correctly)*.

2 A *(well / good)* designed exam tests the students' knowledge *(effectively / effective)*.

3 The examiner marked the tests as *(fair / fairly)* and as *(quickly / quick)* as possible.

4 The coursework on the programme this year was *(unusual / unusually)* *(well / good)*.

5 The students' projects have been of an *(extraordinary / extraordinarily)* *(high / highly)* standard.

Unit **8** Work

Listening — Types of jobs

People at work

 **A**
 **B**
 **C**
 **D**

1 The pictures above show people at work. Match each picture with the person's occupation.

1 farmer .... 2 police officer .... 3 businessman .... 4 doctor ....

2 Complete the definitions with one of the occupations in the pictures.

1 A .... is a person who makes money by selling goods or services.

2 A .... protects the public from criminals.

3 A .... is a person who is qualified in medicine.

4 A person who grows food is called a ....

Extending vocabulary

In the Listening test, the words on the answer sheet may not always be the same as the ones you hear on the recording, so it is important to know as many words as possible that have similar meanings or that are connected with the topic of the recording.

3 Put the verbs in the correct place on the word map on page 57.

look after	defend	supply	earn	take care of
guard	produce		trade	deliver

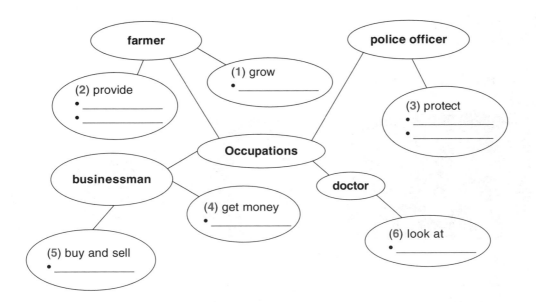

Phrasal verbs

Some verbs change their meaning when they are combined with other words. Phrasal verbs are verbs with two parts, a verb followed by a particle; the particle is usually an adverb or a preposition.

4 Complete the table with the appropriate prepositions.

Verb	Preposition	Meaning
1 look	*for*	search
2 look		care for
3 look		examine
4 look		check
5 look		scan

5 Complete the sentences with the most suitable phrasal verb from the table in Exercise 4.

1 I often .... the newspaper for stories about local companies.

2 The family called the police to help them .... their missing son.

3 My friend is always worried about making mistakes in English and he often asks me to .... his work.

4 When they arrived at the hospital, the doctor .... his broken arm.

5 Will you .... the plants in my office while I'm on holiday?

6 How many phrasal verbs can you make with the verbs below? Make a list and then compare your answers with the phrasal verbs in a dictionary.

make   give   take   get

Vocabulary: Jobs

A

B

C

D

1 Write the missing vowels in the words to make nine occupations.

1 b_s_n_ssm_n	2 ch_f	3 j _ _ rn_l_ist
4 l_wy_r	5 n_rs_	
6 p_l_c_ _ff_c_r	7 p_rs_n_l _ss_st_nt	8 t_ _ch_r
9 v_l_nt _ _ r		

2 Match four occupations from Exercise 1 with photos A–D.

3 Complete the descriptions below with jobs from Exercise 1. Use your dictionary to help you.

1 I'm a .... and I work different shifts each week. My job is to keep people safe.

2 I work for a national newspaper. I interview people and write articles. I'm a ....

3 I help my patients every day. I work in a hospital and I'm a ....

4 I work as a .... I work with animals and I have to look after them every day. I don't get paid for my work.

5 I'm a .... and I work in the city. I have my own company and I make lots of money.

6 I work in a school and my job is to help students pass exams. I'm a ....

4 Listen and check.

5 What do you do? Write a short description of a job you have now or had in the past. (If you are a student, write about someone you know.)

Watch Out!

Learn the correct prepositions.

*I work **in** a hospital / the city / a school.*
*I work **with** animals.*
*I work **for** a national newspaper.*

Vocabulary: Your job

6 Read the different reasons for applying for a job. Which ones are important to you?

to earn a good salary

to help people

to travel the world

to use languages

to work flexible hours

to work for a well-known company

to work in a modern office

to work with different people

7 Listen to three people talking about how they got a job. Which speaker, a, b or c, ...

1 wrote to the company director? ....

2 had a part-time job? ....

3 worked during the summer? ....

4 worked as a volunteer? ....

8 Listen to the three speakers again. Choose the correct options below.

a I had a *part-time / temporary* job at the company and I really enjoyed it. My boss and my colleagues were professional but very friendly. I *volunteered / applied* for a full-time job in my final year at university and I got it. The job is well-paid, so I'm *earning / saving* a good salary, and I also travel to lots of different countries. It's an exciting job.

b I work as a personal assistant at a very well-known *company / office*. I love my job. I got my job last year. I worked here as a volunteer to get *work experience / a qualification*. I really enjoyed it, so I wrote to the company director and asked for a job. I *use my languages / travel the world* regularly and I work *with different people / flexible hours*.

c Two years ago, I worked as a volunteer in a hospital because I wanted to *help people / work with different people*. I went to university, but I worked at the hospital each summer. I didn't want to *travel the world / work in a modern office*, so I applied for the job. Now I'm *working flexible hours / earning a good salary* and it's my dream job!

Watch Out!

*My brother has two **jobs**. He works in a café and he works a fitness instructor.* = specific jobs

*It's difficult for people to find **work** in my country.* = general description

9 Think about a job you (or someone you know) applied for in the past. Write a short description. Include answers to these questions.

- What was the job?
- Where was it?
- Was it a full-time or part-time job?
- Why did you apply for this job?

Grammar: *Have to*

10 Read the rule and look at the table. Then read the interview below and complete the dialogue with the correct form of *have to*.

- *Have to* = there is an obligation or requirement to do something

I / We / You / They	(present) have to	don't have to	work long hours. get a qualification.
	(past) had to	didn't have to	
He / She / It	(present) has to	doesn't have to	
	(past) had to	didn't have to	

A: What do you do?

B: I'm a manager. I work for a well-known international company, so I often (**1**) .... travel to different offices around the world.

A: Did you have to get any qualifications or do any training for your job?

B: Yes, I did. I (**2**) .... complete three training courses. Thankfully, I (**3**) .... revise for any exams because the assessment was an interview and giving a presentation.

A: Do you have to wear a uniform or smart clothes?

B: I (**4**) .... wear a uniform, but I (**5**) .... wear a suit to meetings.

A: Do you have to work long hours?

B: Yes. At the moment, I need to work hard to complete a project.

A: What does your job involve?

B: Well, I (**6**) .... meet lots of people, but I (**7**) .... speak different languages because we all speak English. I often (**8**) .... prepare reports or give presentations.

11 Listen and check.

12 Answer the interview questions in Exercise 9 about your job (or talk about someone you know who has a job).

13 Complete the text with the words below. There is one extra word.

> as   for   salary   to   use   well known   well paid

I really like my job. I work (**1**) .... a part-time manager in a university. I applied for the job last year, and then I had (**2**) .... go for an interview with the manager. We talked about my work experience and why I wanted to work (**3**) .... the university. The university department is very (**4**) .... all over the world and I wanted to (**5**) .... my languages and meet new people. My job isn't (**6**) .... , but I don't have to worry about money because I live with my family.

Reading   Communication at work

1 When starting a company, you need to find ways of letting people know about it. What types of communication has this restaurant used? Label the pictures with the words in the box.

> slogan   advertisement   logo   sign

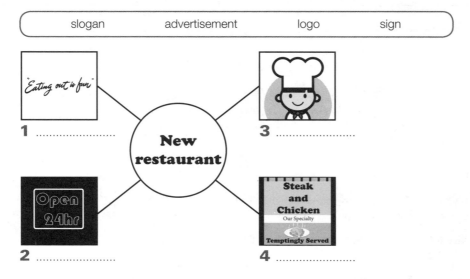

1 ....

2 ....

3 ....

4 ....

2 Read the text on page 61 and underline the words that refer to types of messages. Don't use a dictionary.

It's impossible to avoid advertisements. In our homes, newspaper, magazine and television ads compete for our attention. Posters, billboards and flyers greet us the moment we walk out the door. Advertising agencies stay busy thinking up new ways to get our attention. We have company logos on our clothes. Our email is full of spam, and pop-ups slow us down as we surf the Web. Product placements sneak into films and TV shows. 'Ad wrapping' turns cars into moving signboards. Advertisers have even tried advertising in TV commercials in a subliminal way (affecting your mind without you knowing it). It's no wonder that this is called the consumer age.

3 Find words in the text in Exercise 2 that mean the following:

1 .... : unwanted emails sent to a large number of people, as a way of advertising
2 .... : the practice of a company paying for its product to be placed in a clear position in a film or television programme as a form of advertising
3 .... : very large signs on which posters are displayed
4 .... : a small printed notice, usually distributed by hand, which is used to advertise a particular company, service or event
5 .... : pieces of wood or objects that have been painted with pictures or words and which give some information about a particular place, product or event
6 .... : a person who acquires goods and services for his or her own personal needs
7 .... : a small window containing an advertisement that appears on a computer screen

4 Find words in the text in Exercise 2 that form collocations with the words in the table below.

1	*newspaper*	ads	5		logos
2			6		placements
3			7		commercials
4		agencies	8		age

5 Complete the text with the words below.

> comments   individuals   website   web   corporation   focus   activity

The word 'blog' is a combination of the words (**1**) '.....................' and 'log'. It is a (**2**) .... containing a series of dated entries. A blog can (**3**) .... on a single subject of interest. Most blogs are written by (**4**) .... But sometimes a political committee, (**5**) .... or other group maintains a blog. Many blogs invite readers to leave (**6**) .... on the site. This often results in a community of bloggers who write back and forth to each other. The total group of web logs is the blogosphere. A 'blogstorm' occurs when there is a lot of blog (**7**) .... on a certain topic.

Watch Out!

Articles are small words that can contain a lot of information. Look at these slogans:

Go to work on an egg. (The Egg Council)

The ultimate driving machine (BMW)

The first slogan, which uses the indefinite article *(an)* suggests that any egg will do. The second one uses the definite article *(the)* to suggest that there is only one ultimate driving machine, a car from their specific brand.

6 Do the following nouns relate to general or more specific information? Complete the sentences with **a(n)** or **the**.

1 .... blog can be written by individuals or groups.

2 Within seconds of leaving your house, you will probably see .... advertisement.

3 I quite enjoy watching .... TV commercial for the first time.

4 Technology is very important in .... world of advertising.

5 Yellow is .... colour to be seen in this season.

Writing   Technology at work

1 Match the words and phrases 1–6 that describe things you can do with the words a–f that refer to computers and mobile technology.

1 downloading	a networking	
2 texting or	b an email	
3 sending	c conferencing	
4 social	d music	
5 video	e computer game	
6 playing a	f messaging	

2 To connect two agreeing ideas, we can use linking words such as *in addition, moreover, furthermore* and *also*. Look at the example.

Idea 1	Linking word	Agreeing idea
Computers give employees instant access to company information.	**In addition, Moreover, Furthermore, Also,**	*computers make communication with people in different parts of the company more time effective.*

We can also add an example using *for example*.

*Computers give employees instant access to company information, **for example**, details of projects and how they are progressing.*

Read the essay questions and complete each sentence below with an agreeing idea.

1 *Why is using a computer for long periods of time bad for workers?*

Using a computer for long periods of time is bad for your eyes. In addition,

....

2 *How can technology help us at work?*

Technology at work makes it easier to communicate with other companies.

Furthermore, ...

3 *How can social networking be negative?*

Social networking can be a waste of time. Also, ...

3 To contrast ideas, we can use linking words such as *however, yet, although* and *on the other hand*. Look at the examples.

Idea 1	Linking word	Contrasting idea
Computers give employees access to company information.	**However, On the other hand,**	*if there is a problem with the computer system, it means no one can access the information.*
Computers give employees access to company information	**yet, although**	*not all information on the Internet is correct.*

Read the essay questions and complete each sentence below with a contrasting idea.

1 *Why is using a computer for long periods of time bad for workers?*

Using a computer for long periods of time is bad for your eyes, yet ....

2 *How can technology help us at work?*

Technology makes it easier to communicate with other companies. However, ...

3 *How can social networking be negative?*

Social networking can be a waste of time for some people. On the other hand, ...

Watch Out!

Remember that some linking words (e.g. *However*) must start a new sentence after a full stop. Other linking words (e.g. *although*) join two clauses within one sentence.

I like mobile phones, however I don't like texting. ✗
I like mobile phones. However, I don't like texting. ✓

I like mobile phones. Although I don't like texting. ✗
I like mobile phones although I don't like texting. ✓

4 **Correct the mistakes in the sentences below.**

1 Technology is a good thing because it helps people communicate more easily also it helps people do their jobs more efficiently.

2 People should always pay for music and not download it illegally. Downloading illegally is bad for the music industry. In addition, musicians.

3 Computers have some negative points. It is not always easy to fix a computer if it goes wrong. In addition, there are lots of people who can fix computers.

4 Mobile phones can be dangerous if they are used in a car. However, they can be dangerous for pedestrians who use them when crossing the road.

Unit 9 Holidays and travel

Speaking Types of holidays

Vocabulary: Holidays

A B C D

1 Match the photos A–D with four types of holidays below. Use your dictionary to help you.

activity holiday	beach holiday	city break	coach tour	cruise
family holiday	honeymoon	learning holiday	round-the-world trip	safari

2 Put the words below with the correct verb in the table.

day trips	historical sites	lessons or a course	local festivals
new sports	photos	sightseeing	swimming in the sea
tourist attractions	traditional restaurants	water sports	

do	
eat in	
go	
go on	
learn	
take	
visit	
watch	

3 Write a short description of your last holiday. Use expressions from Exercise 2 to describe what you did.

Vocabulary: Opposite adjectives

4 **Match the adjectives 1–6 with their opposites a–f.**

1 beautiful   a traditional
2 comfortable   b unfriendly
3 delicious   c boring
4 exciting   d horrible
5 friendly   e disgusting
6 modern   f uncomfortable

5 **Complete the sentences with a suitable adjective from Exercise 4.**

1 The beaches were .... and the weather was lovely!

2 We stayed in a .... hotel. It was lovely!

3 I learnt to do water sports. It was .... and I'd like to do it again.

4 We went on a family holiday last year and my mother cooked .... meals.

5 I went on a city break to New York and the people were so ....

6 My sister and I did an English course abroad and the teachers were very ....

7 There was a short bus ride to the hotel, but the journey was really ....

Grammar: Future: *be going to*

6 **Listen to Richard talking about his holiday plans. Which activities is he going to do? Put a ✓ or a ✗ in the table.**

	Richard	my last holiday	my next holiday
1 learn new sports			
2 take lessons			
3 go swimming in the sea			
4 go sightseeing			
5 visit local festivals			
6 eat in traditional restaurants			
7 go on day trips			

7 **Look at the activities in Exercise 6 again and complete the table with your own answers. Put a ✓ or a ✗ for activities you did on your last holiday and activities you are going to do on your next holiday.**

8 **Read the rules and look at the table below. Then look at your answers to Exercise 7 and describe what you are going to do on your next holiday.**

- Use *be going to* + an infinitive.
- Use *be going to* for future plans.

I	'm / am	'm not / am not	going to take lots of photos.
He / She / It	's / is	isn't / is not	
We / You / They	're / are	aren't / are not	going to visit Europe next year.

Pronunciation: /ə/ and sentence stress

 9 Listen to the two sentences below. How is *to* pronounced – strong (with stress) /tu:/, or weak (no stress) /tə/?

1 I'm going **to** study in America.

2 I'm going **to** study in America.

 10 Read and listen to the sentences below. Pay attention to the underlined stressed words. Then listen again and repeat each sentence, copying the pronunciation.

1 I'm going to visit England.

2 I'm not going to visit Spain.

 11 Listen to the sentences below. Underline the stressed words.

1 I'm going to stay in a hotel.

2 I'm not going to take any photos.

3 I'm going to eat in traditional restaurants.

4 We're going to visit historical sites.

5 We're not going to learn a new sport.

6 We're going to go sightseeing.

 12 Listen again to the sentences in Exercise 11 and repeat. Practise the /ə/ sound and using correct sentence stress.

Writing   Where people go on holiday

1 You can use certain verbs to describe changes in the lines on line graphs. Match the verbs below with the lines on these graphs. Write 1, 2, 3 or 4 next to each verb.

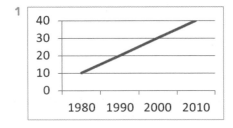

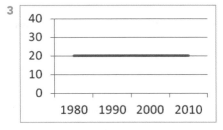

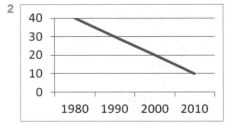

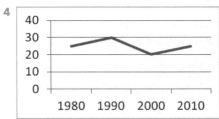

| to increase 1 | to fall | to remain stable | to decrease | to go down |
| to fluctuate | to rise | to drop | to go up | to stay the same |

2 Complete the table with the correct past simple forms of the verbs and any matching nouns.

Infinitive	Past simple	Noun
to increase	increased	1
to rise	2	a rise
to go up	went up	
to decrease	3	a decrease
to fall	fell	4
to go down	5	
to drop	dropped	6
to fluctuate	7	a fluctuation
to remain stable	remained stable	

3 You can use adverbs to describe verbs and adjectives to describe nouns.

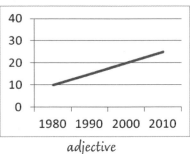

adjective

There was a <u>gradual</u> increase in the number of tourists.

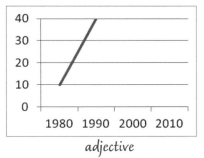

adjective

There was a <u>sharp</u> rise in the number of tourists.

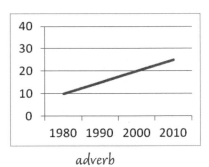

adverb

The number of tourists increased <u>gradually</u>.

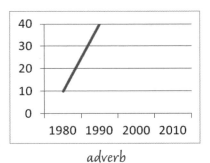

adverb

The number of tourists increased <u>sharply</u>.

Watch Out!

Remember that adjectives come before nouns and adverbs come after verbs.

a rapid (adjective) + *decrease* (noun)

decreased (verb) + *rapidly* (adverb)

Adverbs such as **fast** and **hard** are irregular. (not ~~fastly~~, ~~hardly~~)

4 Complete the sentences about the graphs. Use suitable adverbs or adjectives if possible.

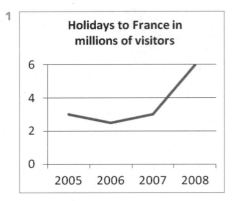

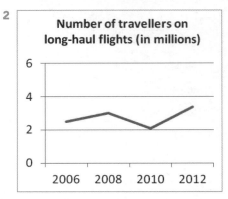

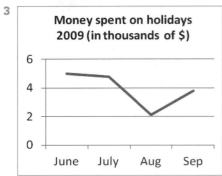

1 There was a _____*sharp increase*_____ in the number of holidays to France in 2008.

2 The number of travellers on long-haul flights _____ between 2006 and 2012.

3 There was a _____ in the amount of money spent on holidays in August 2009.

4 The price of skiing holidays _____ in 2008.

5 You may need to use time expressions to explain when something started or finished, or to explain when something changed. For example:

> **from** 1999 **to** 2012   **between** 2010 **and** 2014   **for** ten years   twenty years **ago**
>
> **in** 2010   **since** 1980   **in** January

Complete the time expressions in the sentences describing graphs 1–4 in Exercise 4.

1 There was a slight increase in holidays to France between 2006 _____ 2007.

2 The number of long-haul flights fluctuated _____ four years.

3 The money spent on holidays remained stable _____ June and July.

4 The price of skiing holidays rose slightly _____ 2005 to 2006.

Nations and nationalities

1 **Quiz: Can you match the countries below with the maps A–D?**

> Malaysia   Portugal   Japan   United Arab Emirates (UAE)

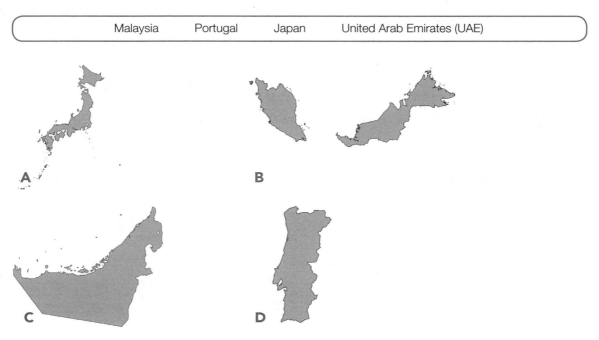

Nationalities are often formed by changing the endings of the names of countries. Look at the examples in the table below. Add the names of the countries below to the appropriate rows. Then complete the nationality column.

> Finland   Venezuela   Yemen   Vietnam   Iran

Country	+ ending	Nationality
Australia	-n	Australian
1		....
Egypt	-ian	Egyptian
2		....
Britain	-ish	British
3		....
Japan	-ese	Japanese
4		....
Pakistan	-i	Pakistani
5		....

2 Complete the sentences about national airlines with the correct nationality.

1 Japan Airlines is a .... airline.

2 Air China is a .... airline.

3 Egyptair is an .... airline.

4 Emirates is an .... airline.

5 TAP Portugal is a .... airline.

6 Malaysia Airlines is a .... airline.

	Departure ↑		↑ 🛄 Bag claim
	Arrival →		🛄 Baggage hall
← Gate 20	Gate 21 →		🛄 Customs control ↗
Connecting Flights	✈↓		Passport control ↗

Terminal 1 →	Gates 1-29 ↑	
	Gates 30-54 ↗	✈
← 🚻 Check-in	Gates 55-79 →	AIRPORT

3 Complete the notes with information from the flight arrivals board below.

Spanish flight arrived at (1) ....

Flight CCA1550 from (2) .... arrived at 6.00.

Emirati flight no (3) .... delayed.

Flight TAP1330 due 7.30 from (4) .... landed Terminal
(5) ....

Flight Arrivals					
Time due	From	Airline	Flight	Terminal	Status
05.00	Madrid	Iberia	IBE0567	50	Arrived 04.50
06.15	Beijing	Air China	CCA1550	15	Arrived 06.00
06.50	Dubai	Emirates	UAE1880	13	Delayed
07.30	Lisbon	TAP	TAP1330	16	Landed

🎧 36 **4** Now listen to a taxi driver talking to a travel agent about the flight arrivals and check your answers.

Reading Getting from place to place

1 **Label the pictures.**

| motorway | country lane | dual carriageway · | path |

1 .... 2 .... 3 .... 4 ....

2 **Circle the best word.**

1 A *runway / motorway / street* is a major road that has been specially built for fast travel over long distances; it has several lanes and special slip roads to enter and exit.

2 A *bridge / pavement / path* is a way between two places that people can walk along.

3 A *main road / dual carriageway / freeway* is the British equivalent for what the Americans call a 'divided highway': a road which has two lanes of traffic travelling in each direction, with a strip of grass or concrete down the middle to separate the two lots of traffic.

4 A *country lane / cycle lane / pavement* is a narrow road, usually in a beautiful location.

3 **Read the blog below about a daily commute (a journey made regularly between one's home and one's place of work). Underline all the phrases that relate to places and circle the ones that refer to travel or transport. Do not use a dictionary.**

commuter101 Is anybody else fed up with roadworks? Is it just here in London where they are appearing all at once, or is it the same everywhere? It's added an hour to my journey. EACH WAY.

Heather98 Pretty much the same here, commuter 101. I have to do a round trip of 120 kilometres between Cheltenham and Birmingham every day and pass (very slowly!) 3 areas with roadworks on different parts of the M5. It's doubling the time it takes me to get to and from work.

Musicfan2 Take a train, guys. Last time I checked, trains were going regularly between Cheltenham and Birmingham. And in London you've got the Tube.

CharlotteL. It's driving me crazy too. There are roadworks near the service station by Junction 9 on the M6. It's like the traffic is at a standstill there. I try to avoid it but it's not always possible.

Heather98 @ Musicfan2: Not an option, I'm afraid. I am a sales rep and need my car during the day.

chico I agree with Musicfan. Instead of complaining about roadworks, the cost of petrol, the price of cars etc. we need to think about other options. And I don't mean car sharing or building more motorways. I say we try to save our environment by campaigning for better bus and train networks and for different types of public transport such as trams. Use your time and anger to try and make a difference!

commuter101 What time? I'm stuck in a traffic jam!! (☺)

4 **Look back at the blog in Exercise 3 and find the following:**

1 a phrase used in informal language that means 'to be tired of something' ....

2 an informal phrase that means 'almost' ....

3 a phrase that means 'a trip to a place and back again' ....

4 the names of two motorways in Britain ....

5 a phrase that refers to places in Britain that sell things such as petrol and oil, but usually also provide toilets and sell food, drink and other goods ....

6 a point on a motorway where traffic may leave or join it ....

7 a word that means 'a complete stop of movement' ....

8 a word that is short for 'representative' ....

9 a word that refers to activities that people carry out over a period of time in order to achieve something such as social, political or commercial change ....

Watch Out!

The language that writers use in texts depends on the readers that they expect. For example, in blogs you will find informal language whereas in journal articles you find formal language. In very informal texts you may also find capitalizations, emoticons (smileys) and exclamations marks (LIKE THIS ☺!). In order to understand texts better, ask yourself what sort of language is being used and who the intended readers of the text are.

5 **Copy and complete the table. Put the words and phrases below into two categories: formal (or neutral) or informal.**

| to be fed up | to commute | almost | pretty much | a rep |
| a campaign | guys | options | anger | a junction |

Formal or neutral	Informal

6 **Match the sentences 1–4 with the type of text a–d they have most likely been taken from.**

1 Nowadays, there is increasing traffic on our roads.

2 The current traffic problems will be analysed with the aid of practical models.

3 The traffic is getting ridiculous ... ARGH!

4 Traffic problems are bringing the UK to a standstill, road organizations have claimed.

a newspaper article

b academic journal article

c student essay

d personal email

Unit **10** Health

Listening — Food and nutrition

| meat | dairy products | vegetables | fruit |

1 Complete the food words with the correct vowels.

1 p_t_t_ _s
2 b_n_n_s
3 c_bb_g_
4 t_rk_y

5 b_ _f
6 ch_rr_ _s
7 ch_ _s_
8 b_tt_r

9 l_mb
10 c_rr_ts
11 p_n_ _ppl_
12 y_gh_rt

2 Complete the table by putting the foods in Exercise 1 into the correct column.

Meat	Dairy products	Vegetables	Fruit

Countable and uncountable nouns

Some nouns can be countable and uncountable. They often become uncountable when they are prepared for eating, e.g.

There are ten chickens in the field. / Would you like some chicken?
I bought two cauliflowers yesterday. / My son doesn't like cauliflower.

3 Say whether the following foods are countable (C), uncountable (U) or both (C/U).

1 carrot   *C/U*
2 rice
3 lamb
4 bean
5 butter
6 onion

7 bread
8 egg
9 pea
10 coffee
11 oil
12 sugar

13 lemon
14 fish
15 chip
16 milk
17 cabbage
18 salad

Cooking terms and methods

4 Match the cooking verbs 1–10 with the phrases a–j.

1 roast ....
2 steam ....
3 fry ....
4 grill ....
5 boil ....
6 bake ....
7 peel ....
8 rub ....
9 pour ....
10 mix ....

a in hot oil
b into a mixing bowl
c the mixture together
d in the oven
e the bread in a hot oven
f the ingredients well
g over boiling water
h directly over the flame
i in hot water
j the potatoes before cooking

Weights and measures

5 Complete the list of ingredients for making pancakes. Choose from the list of weights and measures in the table.

weights (solids)	measures (liquids)
gram (g)	millilitre (ml)
kilogram (kg)	litre (l)

Watch Out!

There are different ways to express numbers, for example 1½ (one and a half) or 1.5 (one point five) kilos. Notice that we use a plural form for anything over one: one **kilo**, but **one and a quarter kilos**; one **litre**, but **one and a half litres**.

Pancakes

1.3 .... *of flour*
10 ...*grams*... *of salt*
300 .... *of sugar*
2 .... *of milk*
450 .... *of cooking oil*
10 *eggs*

6 Complete these equivalents.

¼ = a quarter   ½ = a half   ⅛ = one eighth   ⅓ = a third

(1) .... = three quarters   ⅔ = (2) ....   ⅝ = (3) ....   (4) .... = seven eighths

7 You will hear a list of ingredients. Circle the correct quantity. Then write a different way to express the same quantity.

1 apples   1 kilo / ½ kilo   ....
2 sugar   250 g / 215 g   ....
3 flour   330 g / 130 g   ....
4 butter   120 g / 200 g   ....
5 milk   ⅕ l / 5 l   ....

Speaking | Sport and exercise

Vocabulary: Healthy activities

 A
 B
 C
 D

1 Match the activities below with the photos A–D.

> do sports   eat well   play board games   sleep for eight hours every night

Watch Out!

Use an adverb with a verb.	Don't use an adjective with a verb.
It's important to eat well.	*It's important to eat good.*

2 Complete the table with the activities from Exercise 1 and the activities below.

> do taekwondo   do yoga   draw pictures   have a healthy diet
> play a musical instrument   play brain training games   play table tennis

Good for your mind	Good for your body	Good for both

38 **3** Listen to Jack talking about things he does to keep healthy. Complete the description below.

> brain training games   doing yoga   good for   important to   makes me feel   on my own

I like (1) .... and playing (2) .... I enjoy doing these
activities (3) .... because I work in a busy, noisy office every day. It's
(4) .... relax after a hard day. Yoga (5) .... relaxed
and I think brain training games are (6) .... my mind.

4 Write a short description of something you do to keep healthy. Say:

- what it is
- how often you do it
- where you do it
- who you do it with

Vocabulary: Giving explanations

39 **5** Listen to Charles and Rosa talking about healthy activities they do. What is the activity they like
doing and who do they do it with?

39 **6** Listen again and complete the sentences with the words below.

> happy   hard   keep your mind active

1 It's _____ .

2 It's important to _____ .

3 It makes me feel _____ .

7 Match the words and phrases below to the sentence beginnings in Exercise 6.

> challenging   great   healthy   interesting   keep fit
> relax after college   relaxed   relaxing   work in a team

8 Think of two healthy activities you do and give an explanation about why you like each one. Use the expressions in Exercises 6 and 7 to help you.

1 _____

   _____

2 _____

   _____

Pronunciation: Contractions

9 Circle the contraction (= two words made into one word) in each sentence.

1 It's good for you.

2 It isn't good for you.

3 It's really bad for you.

4 It's important to stay healthy.

5 You shouldn't eat junk food.

40 **10** Listen and repeat the sentence in Exercise 9. Pay attention to the contractions.

Watch Out!

Try to pronounce contractions clearly to make your speaking sound natural. Learning and using contractions will also help you to recognize them when other people are speaking.

Grammar: *Should / shouldn't*

Read the rules. Then choose the correct words to complete the sentences.

- Use *should* or *shouldn't* to make a suggestion.
- Use *should* to say something is a good idea.
- Use *shouldn't to* say something is a bad idea.
- Put *should* and *shouldn't* before the main verb.

11 Circle the correct words.

1 I *should / shouldn't* eat lots of junk food. It isn't good for my body.

2 I *should / shouldn't* try to do more exercise. It's important to stay healthy.

3 Playing the piano makes me feel relaxed. You *should / shouldn't* try it.

4 You *should / shouldn't* study late at night. It's really bad for your health.

5 People *should / shouldn't* play board games like chess. They're good for your mind.

6 You *should / shouldn't* ask your friend to do your homework.

Reading

1 Match the following sports equipment to the pictures.

> bat   racket   board   club

1 .... **2** .... **3** .... **4** ....

2 Can you name two sports that use a racket, two sports that use boards and two sports that use a bat? Use a dictionary to check your ideas.

racket: ....

board: ....

bat: ....

3 Read the definitions 1–4. Which of the games and sports below are being described? Then write a definition for one of the other sports in a similar way.

> cricket   water polo   windsurfing   basketball   golf   netball   tennis   badminton   swimming

1 a game in which a person uses long sticks (called clubs) to hit a small, hard ball into holes that are spread out over a large area of grassy land: ....

2 a game played by two or four players in which the players use a light racket to hit a cone with feathered flights (called a shuttlecock) over a high net: ....

3 a sport in which a person moves along the surface of the sea or a lake on a long narrow board with a sail on it: ....

4 an outdoor game played between two teams in which players try to score points (called runs) by hitting a ball with a wooden bat: ....

4 Do the adjectives below describe positive or negative feelings? Write them in the correct columns. Then use a dictionary to check your answers. Can you add any more words to either column?

> afraid   amazed   amused   angry   annoyed   anxious   ashamed   bored   calm   confident
> curious   delighted   depressed   isappointed   embarrassed   excited   frightened   glad   guilty
> happy   jealous   miserable   nervous   relaxed   sad   terrible   tired   wonderful

Pleasant / Positive feelings	Unpleasant / Negative feelings

Watch Out!

A common mistake is to mix up adjectives ending -ing and -ed, for example *boring / bored* or *amused / amusing*. The -ed ending normally describes feelings, and the -ing ending describes things (often the cause of the feelings).

✗ *The film was long and I was boring.*

✓ *The film was long and it was boring. / The film was long and I was bored.*

---

5 **Complete the sentences with the *-ed* or *-ing* form of the verbs below so that the sentences are true for you. You can use the verbs more than once.**

surprise	frighten	excite	embarrass	satisfy	annoy
disappoint	depress	amaze	tire	amuse	relax

1 In the evening I feel more .... than in the morning.

2 I usually find black and white films ....

3 I have never found any of my exam results ....

4 Classical music makes me feel ....

5 There are still a lot of poor people in the world, which is ....

6 I don't have any .... hobbies.

7 I think animals are ....

8 I don't get easily ....

Writing

Healthcare and lifestyle

1 **Match the pictures to the words in the box.**

  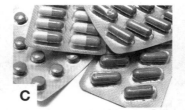 

A   B   C   D

patient	hospital	medicine	doctor

2 **Complete the texts with the words below.**

cure	junk food	medicines	overweight	exercise	illness

Nowadays, many children are (1) .... There are many reasons for this; some people blame the amount of (2) .... that is available, and others claim it is because children don't get enough (3) .... The reality is that childhood obesity is probably a combination of factors.

Doctors have been trying to find a (4) .... for the common cold for years. A cold, which is a relatively harmless (5) ...., can occur at any time of the year and may mean that a person cannot work for days. There are many (6) .... for treating colds but they cannot cure them.

3 **The first conditional is used to show causes and effects in real situations. First conditional structures have two clauses:**

if-clause (condition / cause)	main clause (result / effect)
if + subject + present simple,	subject + *will / can / should / could / might / may* + infinitive without *to*

If my cold gets worse, I will go to bed. **or** *I will go to bed if my cold gets worse.*

Complete the sentences with phrases a–c. Then underline all the result clauses.

a Children might become overweight

b people will have fewer absences from work

c they may live longer

1 If doctors find a cure for the common cold, ...

2 .... if they eat too much junk food.

3 If people exercise every day, ...

4 **The second conditional is used to show causes and effects in unlikely situations. Second conditional structures have two clauses:**

if-clause (condition / cause)	main clause (result / effect)
if + subject + past simple,	subject + *would / could / might* + infinitive without *to*

If all illnesses were cured, everybody would be happy. **or** *Everybody would be happy if all illnesses were cured.*

Use these notes to write second conditional sentences. Keep the information in the order given.

1 Doctors receive better training. Patient care improve.
   If doctors received better training, patient care would improve.

2 Junk food not exist. People not be overweight. ....

3 People live longer. All diseases cured. ....

4 Hospitals free. More people live longer. ....

5 No doctors. A lot more illness. ....

Watch Out!

Remember that there is only <u>one</u> clause with *will / would* in conditional sentences.

If we will eat more fruit, we **will** *be more healthy.* **✗**

If we eat more fruit, we **will** *be more healthy.* **✓**

Taking responsibility

Reading   Rights and responsibilities

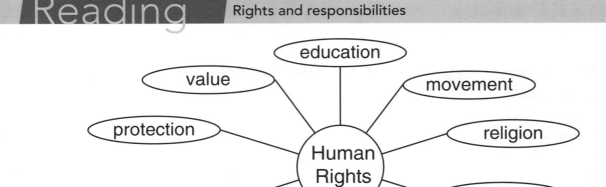

1 The words below are related to professional meetings and responsibilities. Write the words in the correct categories. Use a bilingual dictionary to help you.

minutes (of a meeting)	election	committee	voting	secretary
representative	nomination	member	council	chairperson

A group of people	A person	An object	An activity

2 Complete the text with words from Exercise 1. There may be more than one answer for some of the gaps. You may need to make some words plural.

Beech Lane School Parent (**1**) ....

(**2**) .... of the meeting held on October, 2012

Apologies were received from Mrs Smart.

There were two points covered:

1) Because of the long-term absence of Mrs Smart, we will have a/an (**3**) .... for a new (**4**) .... to lead the meetings. We need all the (**5**) .... two weeks before the next meeting. Any (**6**) .... who attends that meeting will be able to take part in the (**7**) ....

2) The school fair was discussed. A list of duties was drawn up and will be sent to everybody by Friday. It is expected that everyone will do their best to help out on the day.

3 Which words are being defined? Try to write the answers without looking back at Exercise 2.

1 .... : a group of people that controls a group or organization

2 .... : a group of people chosen or appointed to perform a specified service or function

3 .... : a person who handles correspondence, keeps records and does general clerical work for an individual, organization, etc.

4 .... : an official record of the proceedings of a meeting, conference, convention, etc.

5 .... : a person who has authority at a meeting, a committee, a debate, a department, etc.

Watch Out!

In English, the normal word order is subject–verb–object, so we are used to seeing a verb and its subject together. However, sometimes the noun immediately before the verb is not the subject, so when you are skim-reading be careful to look at the whole subject.

The staff members who need to speak to the parents are not here today. (It is not the parents, but the staff members, who need to speak to the parents, who are not here.)

The decision which was made by the school council is not popular. (It is the decision made by the school council, not the school council, that is unpopular.)

4 Read the sentences and answer the questions with the *full* subject. Then underline the most important noun in the subject.

1 *The photographs of the people partying on the beach with my sisters are beautiful.*
Who or what are beautiful?

2 *The importance of the education I received in the UK should not be forgotten.*
What should not be forgotten?

3 *The details of the cases involving the teenagers who travelled without passports are not known yet.*
What is not known?

4 *The secret of a successful career, according to my mother, is to have children first, when you are still young.*
What is this sentence mainly about: the secret, a career or a mother?

Writing

1 Complete the speech bubbles with the words below. Then match each person with the photos A–D.

 A  B  C  D

| abroad | commute | fare | pollution | traffic jams | ~~rush hour~~ | service | crowded |

1 Generally, I like driving, but in the _____*rush hour*_____, when there is a lot of traffic, it can be really frustrating. The roads are really busy here, so there are _____ all the time. `A` `☐`

3 I take the bus to school because the _____ is cheap and there are discounts for students. Also, the _____ is fast and reliable.

2 I work in the city and I _____ to work by underground. It's really quick and easy, but it can also be extremely _____ – I almost never get a seat! `☐` `☐`

4 I often travel _____ with my work, so I spend a lot of time in airports. I like flying, but I worry about the amount of _____ that is caused by the airline industry.

2 Some verbs can be followed by an infinitive with *to* or an *-ing* form.

Verb + infinitive with *to*

I **expect to see** him at the airport.

Everyone **wants to travel** to other countries.

I always **choose to travel** by train.

He **decided to buy** a new car.

I **promise to visit** you next week.

He **appears to be** travel sick!

We **planned to catch** the 10.30 bus.

Verb + *-ing*

I **enjoy travelling** by train.

Some people cannot **resist driving** everywhere.

She **suggested driving** to the airport.

They **considered taking** the underground.

Choose the correct word in each sentence.

1 The government promised not *to increase / increasing* the price of train travel.

2 Many people enjoy *to travel / travelling* by plane.

3 We suggest *to find / finding* alternative sources of fuel.

4 People want *to travel / travelling* cheaply.

5 Oil companies are considering *to raise / raising* petrol prices.

6 The government plans *to change / changing* their policy on air travel.

7 We can expect *to see / seeing* a rise in the number of people who own cars.

8 I have decided *to commute / commute* to work by bus.

3 **Complete the text by putting the verbs in brackets in the correct form.**

Many people (1) ....*enjoy driving*............ (enjoy – drive), but they should try to walk as much as possible. Although using public transport is better than driving, it still pollutes the environment. If everyone (2) .... (decide – walk) at least twice a week, this might have a significant effect on levels of pollution. People who (3) .... (choose – walk) to work or school might also become fitter. People who manage to walk a short distance every day (4) .... (appear – feel) healthier and less stressed. Unfortunately, many people are unable (5) .... (resist – use) their cars because they have busy lives.

4 **To talk about things in general, we often use a noun with zero (no) article or a plural.**

*I try to use **public transport**.* (not ~~the~~ public transport)
***Cars** cause a lot of pollution* (not ~~the~~ cars)

However, with specific nouns, we need an article (*a / an* or *the*).
*Get into **the car**.* (= I know which car.)   *I want to buy **a car**.* (= I don't know which car.)
***The sun** is a long way from **the Earth**.* (= There is only one sun and one Earth in our solar system.)

Complete the sentences with the correct form of the noun in brackets and add the correct article (zero article, *a / an* or *the*).

1 *Trains* .... (train) cause less pollution than cars.

2 .... (pollution) is a common problem in cities.

3 .... (public transport) is a common way of travelling in town.

4 .... (car) are one of the most popular forms of transport.

5 You'll need .... (passport) to travel to other countries.

6 You can book flights and accommodation on .... (Internet).

Vocabulary: Life events

A   **B**   **C**   **D**

1   Match the photos A–D with the events below. There are two extra events.

> coming of age   getting married   getting your first job
> graduating from university   travelling on your own for the first time   winning a sports competition

2   Listen to John talking about one of the events in Exercise 1. Answer the questions below.

1 What was the event?

2 Who was there?

3 How did he feel?

- What was the event?
- Who was there?
- How did you feel?

Watch Out!

Learn the endings of irregular verbs: *feel – felt*

How did he feel?

I felt very excited.

3   Have you experienced one of the events in Exercise 1 or a similar event? How did you feel? Make notes. Then write a short description and record your description.

Vocabulary: Describing feelings

4   Put the adjectives below into the correct group. (Most of the adjectives are in pairs.)

> bored / boring   delighted   excited / exciting   relaxed / relaxing
> satisfied / satisfying   surprised / surprising   terrified / terrifying   tired / tiring

Negative	Positive

5   Listen to Paul talking about an important event. Circle the adjectives from Exercise 4 that you hear.

6 Complete the text with your answers from Exercise 5. Then listen again and check.

I was very nervous before the national championships. I felt (**1**) ....! We travelled to the city the night before and it was a long and (**2**) .... journey on the bus. We were all really (**3**) .... when we woke up the next day. Finally, our match started. I was (**4**) .... because some of the players on my team were very (**5**) .... The opposition were an excellent team and the match was (**6**) ...., but thankfully we won! We were all (**7**) .... and I think our manager was (**8**) .... with the result. It was a really (**9**) .... event for me.

> ### Watch Out!
>
> Use adjectives ending with **-ed** to describe your feelings. *We were all tired*.
>
> Use adjectives ending with **-ing** to describe a thing or an event. *The match was tiring*.

Pronunciation: Giving emphasis

🎧 43 **7** Listen to the sentences. Which word has the most stress in each sentence?

1 I was very bored at my brother's graduation.

2 I feel really tired at the end of the week.

3 I was very surprised when I passed all my exams.

4 I felt really excited when I travelled on my own.

🎧 43 **8** Listen again and repeat. Remember to stress *really* and *very* to give emphasis.

Grammar: Comparing

🎧 44 **9** Listen to Peter comparing different events a student experiences. Match the sentence beginnings 1–4 and the sentence endings a–d. Then listen again and check.

1 I think the most important event	a undergraduates.
2 It is more important than	b taking exams.
3 Graduates are happier than	c for a student is graduation day.
4 Finding a job is more worrying than	d end-of-year exams.

10 Choose the correct word in each sentence.

1 It was the *more / most* exciting day of my life.

2 I think graduation day is a *more / most* important day than your first day at school.

3 In my opinion, studying in your hometown is *better than / best* studying in another town.

4 I really like travelling with friends. It's *more / most* interesting than travelling alone.

5 My *more / most* important event at university was passing my end-of-year exams.

6 I was *happier / happiest* when I passed my driving test than when I passed my exams.

7 The first day in my job was *more / most* worrying than my first day at college.

> ### Watch Out!
>
> Learn the different forms of adjectives.
>
> *good* → *better* (comparative form) → *best* (superlative form)

11 Read the statements below. Do you agree? Change the statements to make them true for you.

1 Studying in your hometown is better than studying in another town or country.

2 People who are getting married are happier than people who are coming of age.

3 Travelling on your own is more boring than travelling with others.

4 Passing a driving test is more exciting than passing exams at school.

5 The most important event for a student is end-of-year exams.

12 Complete the paragraph with the words below. There is one extra word.

boring	felt	happier	most	nervous	than	the	wasn't	younger

For me, I think (1) .... most important event in my life was passing my driving test. I am
(2) .... than all my friends and they all passed their test before me. I remember I was really
(3) .... before each of my driving lessons. I (4) .... very good at the theory because
I found it (5) .... I was (6) .... driving a car (7) .... reading about the rules.
But when the day of the test came, I (8) .... confident.

Listening

Time management

A   B   C   D

1 Match the words below with the photos A–D. There are some words you don't need to use.

career	relaxation	stress	factory	employer	deadline	study

A .... B .... C .... D ....

Words that have similar meanings

2 Circle the word in each list that does <u>not</u> have a similar meaning to the others.

1 career	job	hobby	profession	occupation
2 relaxation	leisure	rest	holidays	work
3 stress	worry	difficulty	pressure	comfort
4 factory	beach	office	shop	workshop
5 employer	boss	owner	worker	manager
6 deadline	limit	goal	target	start

Noun or verb?

3 Some of the words in Exercise 2 are nouns and some are nouns and verbs. Copy and complete the table with the words from Exercise 2. Use a dictionary to check your answers.

Noun	Noun and verb
career	

4 Although the words in Exercise 3 have similar meanings, they are not exactly the same. Complete the sentences with the best word from Exercise 3.

1 Margaret decided to apply for a new .... to earn more money.

2 The college gave the teachers longer .... so they could spend more time with their families.

3 When they are studying for exams, students .... that they will not be able to remember all the important facts.

4 The college organized a day off for the .... staff.

5 The .... of the factory invested in a new building for storing supplies.

6 Students are expected to meet the .... for handing in their work.

Spelling

5 Write the sentences below with the correct punctuation in your notebook.

1 new york is not the Capital of the united states of America.

2 in the uk, children who are born in july usually start school in September, just after they are five

3 oxford university is one of the most famous in the World.

4 in some countries, most companies close on sundays, but in others they close on fridays or saturdays

5 the official language of greece is greek

Watch Out!

Capital letters are part of spelling. You will lose marks in the exam if you do not use capital letters correctly. You should use capitals for:

- the names of countries, towns and cities
- the names of nationalities, religions and languages
- months and days of the week
- the names of institutions and organizations

Unit **12** Money

Shopping options

A   B   C   D

1 **Look at the pictures and match them with the sentences below.**

1 There are supermarkets in most big cities across the world. ....

2 People who live in small towns often buy their food at the market. ....

3 In the countryside, people often get their groceries in village shops. ....

4 Department stores sell clothes, furniture and household goods. ....

2 **Complete the sentences with the expressions below.**

> designer brands   shop assistant   customer services   shopping malls   market stalls   self-service

1 Ingrid complained to .... about her new boots because the zip was broken.

2 A lot of teenagers like expensive .... more than cheap clothes.

3 One advantage of .... is that you can choose your own food from the shelves.

4 Many young people in big cities go to .... to meet their friends.

5 Farmers often sell their fruit and vegetables from ....

6 The .... helped the customer to find a T-shirt in the colour they wanted.

45 **3** **Listen to the following sentences and underline the stressed words.**

1 I bought this shirt in a sale.

2 My brother thinks online shopping is much quicker than going to the shops.

3 The good thing about shopping in a department store is that you can get everything in one place.

4 The last time I took something back to a shop, the customer services manager wasn't there.

5 I lost my credit card the other day. I was really worried someone else would use it.

6 Have you ever bought a train ticket with a student discount? It's so much cheaper.

4 Match the verbs 1–5 with the nouns a–e to form expressions about shopping.

1 go   **a** the shopping

2 ask for   **b** a shopping list

3 make   **c** the supermarket

4 do   **d** shopping

5 go to   **e** a refund

5 Now listen to a recording of an interview in a survey of shopping habits. Miriam is talking about who does the shopping in her family. Complete the notes with expressions from Exercise 4.

- Four people in the family – only two **(1)** ....
- Mother buys the food. Makes a **(2)** .... first.
- Goes to **(3)** .... weekly.
- Miriam **(4)** .... most. Sometimes buys clothes she doesn't like. Takes them back and asks for **(5)** ....

Speaking   Possessions

Vocabulary: Objects

A   B   C   D

1 Look at the photos A–D above. Which of the objects do you own? Which would you like to own? Why?

2 Match some of the words below to the objects in the photos A–D.

black   glass   large   leather   metal   modern   new   old-fashioned   plastic   red   gold   small   wood

3 Put the words from Exercise 2 in the correct column in the table below.

Size	Age	Colour	Material

4 Listen to two people talking about their favourite possessions. What are they? Which words do they use to describe the objects?

Watch Out!

Put adjectives in the correct order:
(1) size, (2) age, (3) colour, (4) material.

a small, new, brown, leather bag

5 Choose one of the objects in the photos in Exercise 1 or an object you own and make notes on the points below:

- size
- age
- colour
- material
- why you like it

Vocabulary: Describing objects

6 Match the sentence beginnings 1–6 with the groups of endings a–f.

1 I wear it   a cotton / glass / metal.

2 I got it for   b carrying all my things / downloading music / studying and reading.

3 It's made of   c my birthday / my graduation / my wedding.

4 It's important to me because   d a brilliant holiday / a special day / my country.

5 I use it for   e every day / for special occasions / when I go on long trips.

6 It reminds me of   f I bought it on my first trip overseas / I saved up to buy it / my best friend gave it to me.

7 Complete the descriptions below with the sentence beginnings 1–6 in Exercise 6.

1 One of my favourite possessions is my laptop. .... chatting online or watching films with my friends.

2 I wear this necklace every day. .... my wedding day because my husband bought it for me. It's very special.

3 I have a very large suitcase. I've had it since I was eighteen. .... I bought it for my first trip to America.

4 My mobile is important to me. It's small and .... metal and plastic. It's got lots of things on it – music, apps, photos and Internet.

8 Look back at your notes from Exercise 5. Use the notes and the phrases from Exercise 6 to write a description.

Pronunciation: Linking words

 9 Read and listen to the sentences below. Pay attention to the link ‿ between the two words.

1 It's made of leather.

2 I use it for texting my friends.

3 I like it because

4 It's important to me because

5 It reminds me of

 10 Listen again and repeat each sentence. Complete each sentence with your own ideas.

Watch Out!

Learning how to link consonant sounds and vowel sounds in your sentences will help you to speak at a natural pace.

Grammar: Present perfect with *for* and *since*

11 Listen and complete the sentences with the correct past participles and *for* or *since*.

1 I've .... my mobile .... about three months.

2 I've .... this guitar .... 2002.

3 I've .... this laptop .... a year.

4 I've .... this photo in my bag .... my graduation.

5 I've .... this watch .... years.

6 I've .... a new car .... I passed my driving test.

12 Answer the questions below. Use the present perfect with *for* or *since* in your answers. What important object have you ...

- owned since you were a child?
- used for years?
- had for a few months?
- wanted since you were a teenager?

Watch Out!

Use the past simple for a finished event in the past.

I bought it last year.

13 Complete the text with the words below. There are two extra words.

> bought   carry   favourite   had   important   it   green   modern   possessions   reminds   wear

I've got lots of really great (**1**) .... But I think my (**2**) .... possession is my coat. I got (**3**) .... for my graduation to celebrate getting my degree. I've (**4**) .... it for two years. My parents (**5**) .... it for me and I was really surprised. It's beautiful. It's a (**6**) .... , black, leather coat. It's (**7**) .... to me because I know my parents were very proud of me. It (**8**) .... me of studying for my degree and my time at university. I only (**9**) .... it for special occasions because it's really expensive.

Writing   Money and happiness

1 Decide if the words below are nouns (N), verbs (V) or adjectives (A). Write N, V or A. (One word can have two labels.) Then match the words to the definitions.

> wealth   spend   save   rich A   possessions   inherit
> salary   tax   poverty   wealthy   savings   income

1 money that the government takes from you .... *tax* ....

2 money that you keep for the future ....

3 money that you receive from your employer ....

4 the noun for being poor ....

5 an adjective to describe rich people ....

6 money that you receive from work, rent or investments ....

7 things that you own ....

2 Complete what Fariba says with words from Exercise 1.

Fariba

In my country people do not pay much money to the government in
(**1**) .... In general, most people earn a good
(**2**) .... from their jobs and we make sure we
(**3**) .... enough money for the future. Some
people are (**4**) .... and live in large houses and
own expensive cars. These people (**5**) .... a lot
of money on possessions. Some of their (**6**) ....
comes from renting flats to other people and from business
investments.

3 Pronouns are used to refer to nouns that have already been mentioned. Using pronouns helps you avoid repetition, connects your sentences together and makes your writing more fluent.

Money is necessary to live. *It* *pays for accommodation, food and clothing. (It = money)*
People who do not have a lot of money *can be happy.* *They* *can be happy for other reasons. (They = people who do not have a lot of money)*

You can use *this* to refer to ideas.
The number of wealthy people is increasing in some parts of the world. *This* *is good for the economy.*
(This = The number of wealthy people is increasing in some parts of the world.)

Complete the sentences with one of the pronouns below.

> It   they   this

1 <u>People who enjoy their work are often happy</u>. ____*This*____ means they often work harder and are better employees.

2 Happiness comes in many different forms. For some people .... comes from work. For others .... comes from enjoying life.

3 The main reason people want to earn money is to improve their life. For example, ... might want to have more possessions.

4 Good weather can have an effect on people's happiness. .... makes them feel more positive and less stressed.

5 Children often make a couple happier. .... help adults focus on the most important things in life.

6 People who inherit a lot from their parents can become wealthy overnight. .... makes their lives much easier because .... no longer have to worry about their future income.

Now underline the noun or idea that each pronoun refers to. (The first one has been done as an example.)

4 Sometimes we use *this / these* + noun to refer to an idea / different ideas.

People who have a negative attitude to life can be very unhappy. *This problem* *can affect everyone. Taxes have increased, salaries have been cut and food prices have risen.* *These factors* *have led to a drop in living standards across the region.*

Complete the sentences with *this* or *these* and the nouns (singular or plural) below.

> approach   action   problem   change

1 When governments raise or lower taxes, the income of citizens can increase or decrease. .... have an effect on the wealth or poverty of a whole nation for many years.

2 Talking about money problems can help people understand how to manage them better in the future. .... is often used by counsellors.

3 Giving advice or gifts and lending money to friends are common in all cultures. ....
help to increase the bonds between people.

4 It is difficult to know how much money to save for the future. .... is common for
many families with children.

Now underline the verbs after the added nouns. Are they singular or plural? Write S or P next to sentences 1–4 above.

Watch out!

Make sure pronouns and verbs agree in number with the nouns they refer back to.

Reading   Running a business

1   Match the words 1–9 with their definitions a–i.

1 withdrawal

a if you have this, you have spent more money than you have in your bank account, and so you owe the bank money

2 pension

b an amount of money that you take from your bank account

3 pay slip

c a sum of money that you pay to be allowed to do something

4 overdraft

d a small piece of paper that shows how much an employer has paid you

5 mortgage

e a regular sum of money received after retiring (retire = stop work completely), given by an employer or by the state

6 current account

f a punishment in which a person is ordered to pay a sum of money because they have done something illegal or broken a rule

7 cheque

g a printed form on which you write an amount of money and who it is to be paid to. Your bank then pays the money to that person from your account

8 fee

h a personal bank account that you can take money out of at any time using your cheque book or cash card

9 fine

i a loan of money which you get from a bank or building society in order to buy a house

2 Copy and complete the table with the words that relate to the categories. Some words relate to more than one category.

> ATM   withdrawal   cash point   salary   rent   purchase   pay slip
> overdraft   loan   investment   hole in the wall   fees   debit card   savings account
> fines   mortgage   credit card   cheque   automatic teller machine   owe

Saving money	Borrowing money from the bank	Getting your own money from the bank	Earning money	Paying money

3 Now underline four phrases in the category 'Getting your own money from the bank' that have the same meaning.

4 Complete these sentences using words from Exercise 2.

1 I have to go to the _____ before we go to the restaurant.

2 If you want to avoid paying a _____, you need to pay your taxes in time.

3 If your children attend private school, you need to pay school _____.

4 The bank has given me an _____: if I owe them less than £100 they won't charge me interest.

5 When I moved, I took out a _____ over 25 years, but I hope to pay it back early.

Watch Out!

Although *few* and *a few* both mean 'not many', they are used quite differently.

Few has a negative meaning. It emphasizes what is missing.

*There are **few** copies of this book.* = Not many copies exist, so you may not get one.

A few means 'a small number'. It emphasizes what is (still) there.

*There are **a few** copies of this book.* = There aren't many copies but there are some, so you can still have one.

Note that *few* is normally used in a formal context.

5 Match the sentences 1–2 with their meaning a–b.

1 It should be noted that **there are <u>a few</u> theorists who believe that** this is the right way to do business.

2 It should be noted that **there are <u>few</u> theorists who believe that** this is the right way to do business.

a There are some theorists who believe that.

b It is difficult to find a theorist who believes that.

Answer key

Unit 1 Family Speaking

Exercise 1
1 sister
2 brothers
3 parents
4 mother, wife
5 daughter, sons
6 grandparents, husband

Exercise 2
1 sister
2 brother
3 mother
4 father

Exercise 5
brother   mother   grandmother

Exercise 6
bossy, calm, clever, confident, creative, friendly, funny, happy, kind
Students' own answers

Exercise 7
1 clever
2 bossy
3 confident
4 calm
5 friendly, funny

Exercise 8
Speaker 1: kind, creative   Speaker 2: clever
Speaker 3: bossy, funny

Exercise 9
Speaker 1: looks   Speaker 2: brothers
Speaker 3: favourite

Exercise 11
1 Our
2 Their
3 His
4 Her
5 her
6 my
7 Its
8 your

Exercise 12

I	you	he	she	it	we	they
my	your	his	her	its	our	their

Listening

Exercise 1
a 2   b 3   c 4   d 1

Exercise 2
2 presentation   present   present
3 suggest   suggestion
4 project   project   projector
5 inform   information
6 explain   explanation

Exercise 3
1 introduction
2 suggest
3 present (v)
4 project (n)
5 information
6 explain

Exercise 4
diagram: chart, graph, plan, table
picture: icon, image, photograph
subject: area, issue, theme, topic

---

advantages: benefits, good points, pros
disadvantages: bad points, cons, dangers

Reading

Exercise 1
1 C   2 B   3 A

Exercise 2
A nuclear family   C extended family
B single-parent family

Exercise 3
1 f   4 b   7 k   10 i
2 j   5 e   8 a   11 g
3 l   6 d   9 c   12 h

Exercise 4

Female	Male	Either
mother-in-law	brother	divorcee
widow	husband	parent
wife	son-in-law	stepchild
		sibling

Exercise 5
1 widower
2 husband
3 couple
4 household
5 an arranged
6 siblings
7 parents-in-law
8 stepchildren

Writing

Exercise 1
1 mother
2 son
3 daughter
4 father
5 grandmother
6 mother-in-law
7 grandson
8 parents

Exercise 2
2 must
3 should
4 shouldn't
5 don't need to
6 might

Exercise 3
2 I will go to university in the future.
3 Parents shouldn't smoke near their children.
4 Children might / could have lessons on the Internet in the future.
5 Children must / have to / need to be learn basic skills like maths and reading.

Exercise 4
1 Children who don't study might / could fail their exams.
2 University should prepare people for good jobs.
3 Children should follow their parents' advice.

Unit 2 Leisure Listening

Exercise 1

Hobbies	Interests	Sports
5 painting	2 going to the theatre	1 cycling
6 stamp collecting	3 watching TV	4 fencing

Exercise 2

Hobbies	Interests	Sports
stamp collecting	going to the cinema	cycling
cooking	going to art galleries	football
gardening	listening to music	running
painting	playing chess	swimming
	travelling	

Exercise 3
Conversation A Speaker 1: swimming
Speaker 2: running
Conversation B Speaker 1: going to the cinema   Speaker 2: going to a concert
Conversation C Speaker 1: travelling
Speaker 2: gardening
Conversation D Speaker 1: cycling
Speaker 2: cooking

Exercise 4
1 to   3 two   5 to
2 too   4 too   6 two

Speaking

Exercise 1
A playing computer games   B reading magazines
C jogging   D going shopping

Exercise 2
doing: exercise, nothing
going: for walks, to the gym
playing: football, tennis
watching: a DVD, TV

Exercise 5
Speaker 1: using the Internet, playing computer games
Speaker 2: doing nothing, reading magazines
Speaker 3: going shopping, going for walks

Exercise 6
1 I love
2 I really like
3 I prefer
4 I don't like
5 It depends.
6 My favourite thing

Exercise 8
1 a   2 b   3 b   4 a   5 a

Reading

Exercise 1
2 sharing　3 having fun　4 chatting

Exercise 2
1 sharing
2 Partying
3 Chatting
4 having fun

Exercise 3

Play	Go	Do
basketball	dancing	exercise
board games	hiking	karate
cards	shopping	kick boxing
chess	skiing	puzzles
snakes and ladders	swimming	sports
tennis		weightlifting
		yoga

1 go　　2 play　　3 do

Exercise 4
Jack, 15: I spend time with my family most evenings. At the weekend, I prefer to hang out with my friends at the park or in the playground in the local woods. If it rains, I like to go to see a film with my friends.

Monica, 18: I belong to a chess club that meets twice a month, and once a year we go camping. It's the highlight of my summer! We stay in tents on a lovely camp site and have picnics and barbecues. In the evenings, we organize quizzes and play cards. And we also play a lot of chess, of course!

Amrita, 12: My older sisters spend a lot of time with their friends in the local shopping centre, but I'm not allowed to go out without an adult yet. I can still chat to my friends all the time, though, by phone, email or text message.

Exercise 5
1 shopping centre
2 adult
3 camp site
4 picnic
5 barbecues (singular: barbecue)
6 quizzes (singular: quiz)

Writing

Exercise 1
2 watch TV
3 go swimming / swim
4 listen to music

Exercise 2
Do: gymnastics, karate, sports, yoga
Go: horse riding, shopping, skating, swimming
Play: computer games, football, golf, sports, the guitar, the violin
Watch: football, golf, gymnastics, horse riding, karate, skating, sports, swimming, TV

Exercise 3
2 play
3 plays
4 play
5 playing
6 plays
7 play
8 doesn't / does not play
9 play
10 plays
11 don't / do not play

Exercise 4
0 no　not much/not many/few　some　a lot of　all 100
2 All
3 No
4 Some / A lot of
5 Few / Not many

Unit 3 Different cultures Speaking

Exercise 1
A family, balloons, cake
B fireworks
C carnival, costume

Exercise 2
1 give　4 presents　7 watch
2 make　5 parade　8 fireworks
3 family　6 wear

Exercise 3
1 d　2 f　3 c　4 e　5 b　6 a

Exercise 4
1 but　3 too　5 because
2 then　4 After　6 When

Exercise 5
1 ate　3 made　5 wore
2 gave　4 met　6 saw

Exercise 6
1 went　3 was
2 graduated　4 danced
5 didn't stay
6 were

Exercise 8
/t/: liked, walked
/d/: loved, studied
/id/: started, wanted

Exercise 9
1 met
2 watched
3 travelled
4 but
5 wore
6 played
7 when
8 saw

Reading

Exercise 1
1 c　2 a　3 d　4 b

Exercise 2
1 The Gherkin
2 The Palace of Westminster
3 City Hall
4 The Old Bailey

Exercise 3
1 kettle
2 cup
3 tearoom
4 teapot
5 jam
6 customs
7 butter
8 sandwiches
9 salmon
10 milk

Exercise 4
Food
- Cornish pasty (a pastry case with a filling of meat and vegetables)
- scones (light plain cake made from flour with very little fat, cooked in an oven, usually split open and buttered)
- haggis (a dish made from sheep's or calf's offal, oatmeal and suet, boiled in a skin made from the animal's stomach)
- rarebit (melted cheese sometimes mixed with milk and seasonings on toast)
- leek (a vegetable belonging to the onion family)

Drink
- barley water (a drink made from an infusion of barley, usually flavoured with lemon or orange)
- Irn-Bru (a Scottish carbonated drink)

Activity
- duck-duck-goose (a circle games based on chasing each other)
- hopscotch (a children's game that involves jumping between squares that are drawn on the ground)
- British bulldog (a running game in which people try to run from one end of an area to another without being caught by two people: the 'bulldogs')

Exercise 5

Scotland	Wales	England
haggis	rarebit	Cornish pasty
Irn-Bru	leek	scones

Exercise 6

Ireland is the island which includes Northern Island and the Republic of Republic.

England, Wales and Scotland together make up Great Britain.

The UK consists of Great Britain and Northern Ireland.

Listening

Exercise 1
Across:
3 national
4 huts

Down:
1 Chinese
2 Italy

Exercise 2
1 pronunciation
2 alphabet
3 spicy
4 vegetarian
5 scarf
6 silk
7 brick
8 block of flats

Exercise 3
1 diet
2 housing
3 communication
4 costume

Exercise 4

scarf, vegetarian, pronunciation, brick

Exercise 5

1	have	3	done	5	do
2	made	4	had	6	have

Writing

Exercise 1

A architecture	C a concert
B a museum	D an art gallery

2 A concert **3** Architecture **4** An art gallery

Exercise 2

useful P interesting P tiring N creative P
amazing P beautiful P harmless P
terrible N

A: 2 beautiful / interesting **3** tiring

B: 1 interesting **2** dangerous **3** harmless
4 terrible

Exercise 3

2 Louise gave me a bestselling book for my
birthday.

3 My sister and I saw a Shakespeare play in
London.

4 Tokyo has many interesting art galleries
nowadays.

5 Older people like opera more than young
people.

6 Most teenagers listen to music on the Internet.

Unit 4 Places to live Speaking

Exercise 1

A harbour	C market
B shopping mall	

Exercise 2

Suggested answers

harbour: go on a boat trip, have a coffee

shopping mall: buy clothes, have a coffee

market: have a coffee

Exercise 3

Model answers

1 cafe, gallery, hotel (restaurant), theatre
2 beach, park, river (harbour)
3 beach, cafe, gallery, park, theatre (cinema)
4 cafe, factory, gskyscraper (office)
5 bridge, skyscraper (hill)

Exercise 4

1 c	2 a	3 e	4 d	5 b

Exercise 5

Model answers

1 modern, beautiful
2 airport, mountains
3 museums, lots of tourist attractions
4 museums, traditional food
5 the weather is good

Exercise 7

One syllable: beach, bridge, park
Two syllables: café, hotel, river
Three syllables: factory, gallery, skyscraper, theatre

Exercise 8

Two syllables: ca<u>fé</u>, <u>ho</u>tel, <u>ri</u>ver
three syllables: <u>fac</u>tory, <u>gal</u>lery, <u>sky</u>scraper,
<u>the</u>atre

Exercise 9

There's (a) museum, (lots of) traffic
There isn't (a) beach, (any) accommodation
There are (some) shopping malls, (lots of)
people, markets
There aren't (any) harbours

Exercise 10

1	are	3	are not	5	No	7	aren't
2	isn't	4	Are	6	are		

Exercise 11

1	near	5	bridge	9	meet
2	famous	6	favourite	10	are
3	got	7	can		
4	skyscrapers	8	traditional		

Writing

Exercise 1

2 sports centre **3** shopping centre
4 entertainment complex **5** business park
6 industrial area

Exercise 2

2	e	4	f	6	g	8	a
3	b	5	c	7	h		

Exercise 3

1	convert	5	reduced
2	expanded	6	growing
3	altered	7	deteriorated
4	improve	8	transforming

Exercise 4

2 highest
3 lowest
4 entertainment complexes
5 the largest

Reading

Exercise 1

1	centre	3	policing	5	care
2	college	4	service	6	spirit

Exercise 2

communal: adjective; **c** belonging or relating to a
community as a whole; something that is shared

a commune: noun; **b** a group of people who live
together and share everything

a communist: noun; **a** a supporter of
communism (the political belief that all people are
equal and that workers should control the means
of producing things)

Exercise 3

criminal adjective ✓; verb: to criminalize
(note: we say 'to commit' a crime);
adverb: criminally; noun ✓

volunteer adjective: voluntary; verb ✓;
adverb: voluntarily; noun: ✓

loyalty adjective: loyal; verb: (to be loyal);
adverb: loyally; noun: ✓

residential adjective ✓; verb: to reside
adverb: –; noun: residence, resident

punish adjective: punishable, punishing; verb: ✓
adverb: –; noun: punishment

Exercise 4

1 a – political party
2 f – online community
3 g – voluntary organization
4 b – film cast
5 c – rock band

6 d – friendship group
7 e – sports team

Listening

Exercise 1

1	library	3	halls of residence
2	sports centre	4	medical centre

Exercise 2

1	sports centre	3	library
2	medical centre	4	halls of residence

Exercise 3

1	through	3	restaurants	5	until
2	There	4	foreign	6	twelfth

Exercise 4

1	into	3	outside	5	between
2	far away	4	behind		

Exercise 5

1	E	3	C	5	A
2	D	4	B		

Unit 5 Arts and media Writing

Exercise 1

2	action	5	horror film
3	documentary	6	science fiction
4	thriller		

Exercise 2

2	soundtrack	5	genres
3	story	6	blockbusters
4	effects		

Exercise 3

1 documentary; story
2 science fiction; special effects
3 genre; soundtracks; horror

Exercise 4

25 per cent = a quarter
75 per cent = three quarters
33 per cent = a third
66 per cent = two thirds

Exercise 5

1 A third of adults do not watch science fiction
films.

2 Ten per cent of worldwide film sales come
from Bollywood.

3 Three quarters of people over 65 watch films
on television.

4 Ninety per cent of children watch cartoons on
a regular basis.

Exercise 6

1 c	2 d	3 b	4 a

Reading

Exercise 1

1	a guide	3	a biography	5	a journal
2	a comic	4	a dictionary	6	a mystery

Exercise 2

1 drawings
2 daily activities
3 the same subject or characters

4 another person
5 book

Exercise 3
Fiction: a comic, a mystery
Non-fiction: a dictionary, a guide, a journal, a biography

Exercise 4
1 d   **2** b   **3** c   **4** a

Exercise 5
1 biography / autobiography
2 autobiography / biography
3 dialogues
4 mystery

Speaking

Exercise 1
1 B   **4** A
2 extra description   **5** extra description
3 C   **6** D

Exercise 3
a Speaker 1   c Speaker 2
b Speaker 3

Exercise 4
a Speaker 1   e Speaker 1
b Speaker 3   f Speaker 3
c Speaker 1   g Speaker 3
d Speaker 3   h Speaker 2
It's very exciting.
I think it's good entertainment.
The thing I like best is the hotel manager.

Exercise 6
1 e   **2** f   **3** c   **4** d   **5** a
6 b

Exercise 7
1 rarely   **2** often   **3** always

Exercise 8
1 favourite, every, contestants, by
2 about, interesting, operas, actors
3 series, always, stars, exciting
4 talk, funny, contestants, sometimes

Listening

Exercise 1
Tick: break into, thief, gun, pickpocket

Exercise 2

Noun	Verb	Adjective
crime	steal	dangerous
knife	rob	careful
gun	break into	safe
gang	attack	
thief		
safe		

Exercise 3
1 burglar, stole (past tense)   **2** pickpocket

3 shoplifter   **5** safe
4 gang, robbers (plural)

Exercise 4
1 e   **2** c   **3** a   **4** b   **5** d

Exercise 5
1 called the police   **4** watch out for
2 crime scene   **5** take them to court
3 locked up

Exercise 7
When the receptionist arrived at Goodmead Primary School on Monday, she found that someone had broken into the office and stolen several laptops, so she called the police.

Unit 6 The natural world Speaking

Exercise 1
A rainy, wet   C stormy, windy
B cold, snowy   D hot, sunny

Exercise 2
A rainy, wet   C stormy, windy
B cold, snowy   D hot, sunny

Exercise 4
1 favourite   **4** makes
2 There's   **5** lasts
3 it's   **6** really like

Exercise 7
/uː/ humid, June
/aʊ/ drought, outside
/ʌ/ month, sunny
/eɪ/ April, rainy
/ɔː/ autumn, stormy
/əʊ/ November, snowy

Exercise 9
1 can   **3** can't   **5** can't
2 can't   **4** can   **6** can

Exercise 11
1 season, it's, can, makes
2 monsoon, for, can't, dry
3 There's, can, from, thunderstorms

Listening

Exercise 1
Suggested answers

Picture 1	Picture 2	Picture 3	Picture 4
oil rig	natural gas	trawler	underwater turbine
natural gas	mineral resource	fish farm	wave power
mineral resource	gas pipeline	net	energy
off-shore drilling	energy		
energy	fuel		
fuel			

Exercise 2
1 e   **2** d   **3** b   **4** c   **5** a

Exercise 3
1 Oil is a non-renewable source of energy.
2 Trawlers sometimes spend many months at sea.
3 Off-shore drilling has affected wildlife in this area.
4 We need fuel for our car.
5 Underwater turbines capture energy from ocean currents.

Exercise 4
The graphs show trends.
1 d   **2** a   **3** b   **4** c

Exercise 5
Suggested answers

Statistics	Trends
average (noun /adjective)	rise (noun / verb)
per cent (noun)	gradual (adjective)
more than (adjective)	fall (noun / verb)
majority (noun)	increase (noun / verb)
minority (noun)	decrease (noun / verb)
less than (adjective)	remain stable (verb + adjective)
fraction (noun)	downward (adverb / adjective)
number (noun)	upward (adverb / adjective)
slight (adjective)	tendency (noun)
amount (noun)	dramatic (adjective)
significant (adjective)	

Writing

Exercise 1
2 i   **4** a   **6** b   **8** c   **10** h
3 g   **5** j   **7** f   **9** d

Exercise 2
1 temperature   **3** harvest
2 pollution   **4** erupted

Exercise 3
2 seeds are watered   **5** flowers are picked
3 plants grow   **6** plants die
4 plants flower

Exercise 4
2 is eaten; are eaten   **5** are damaged
3 are destroyed   **6** is caused
4 are inhabited

Exercise 5
2 Chemicals are used by farmers to protect plants from insects.

3 Seeds are planted in the spring.

4 Elephants and camels are used as working animals in some countries.

5 Volcanoes and other natural disasters ~~is~~ are studied by scientists.

6 Fields ~~be~~ are watered by a special system called irrigation.

Reading

Exercise 1
1 waterfall **2** valley **3** bay **4** cliff

Exercise 2
1 land **2** sand **3** ground **4** soil

Exercise 3
Suggested answers
Our knowledge of Natural History would not be what it is today without the work of women explorers, artists and scientists. In this leaflet, you will learn about three British pioneering women, among the first to be involved in uncovering some of the rich history of the natural world.

Mary Anning (1799–1847)
Mary came from a poor family who lived in Lyme Regis, a town on the south-west coast of England. Her father tried to make extra money by selling fossils (plant and animal remains in rocks) to rich tourists. Consequently, Mary and her siblings learned from an early age how to look for fossils, although she was the only one of the brothers and sisters who became an expert. However, in her lifetime she did not always get the credit she deserved as it was male geologists who published the descriptions of any finds. Her important finds include the first skeleton of an ichthyosaur, or fish-lizard, a plesiosaur, also known as sea-dragon, and a pterodactyl, or 'flying dragon'.
Collecting fossils on the cliffs was dangerous work. Mary's dog Tray was killed when rocks and earth fell down a cliff, and she nearly lost her life in the same landslide.

Dorothea Bate (1878–1951)
Born in the Welsh countryside, she had a passion for natural history from an early age. She became the first female scientist in the Natural History Museum in London. She was a palaeontologist, that is, a scientist who studies fossils in order to understand the history of life on Earth. She went to mountains and cliffs in the Mediterranean and explored hilltops in Bethlehem, discovering and documenting animal fossils. She wrote hundreds of reports, reviews and papers.

Evelyn Cheesman (1881–1969)
Although Evelyn wanted to become a veterinary surgeon, this was not possible for women in the early twentieth century. Instead, she trained as a canine nurse.
Her first job, however, was not related to dogs: she worked in the insect house at the London Zoological Society. She was very adventurous and went on many expeditions to remote locations, as far away as the Galapagos Islands. Despite being very busy, she managed to publish 16 books.

Exercise 4
Lyme Regis – a town on the south-west coast of England
fossils – plant and animal remains in rocks
siblings – brothers and sisters
ichthyosaur – fish-lizard
plesiosaur – sea-dragon
pterodactyl – flying dragon
Tray – Mary's dog

landslide – rocks and earth [falling] down a cliff
palaeontologist – a scientist who studies fossils in order to understand the history of life on Earth
canine – related to dogs
remote – far away

Exercise 5
1 ✓ There is a contrast between 'no evidence' and what people believe.

2 ✗ Both sentences support the same information.

Unit 7 Education Writing

Exercise 1
1 class   4 lectures
2 cteacher   5 presentation
3 exam

Exercise 2

Verbs	Nouns
take / sit / do / pass / fail / write	an exam
get	a qualification
do / take / pass / fail	a course
write / do	an essay
study / do / pass / fail	a subject
give / make / do	a presentation

1 passed
2 study / do
3 take / sit / do / write / pass
4 write / do
5 give / make / do
6 sit / take / do / write / pass
7 get

Exercise 3
1 took   **3** have   **5** do   **7** do
2 give   **4** get   **6** get **8** give

Exercise 4
1 Fourteen, went   4 Thirty-four, continued
2 One, started
3 Five, eight, found   5 thirteen, didn't go
                        6 Eight, decided

Exercise 5
the same, less, larger, smaller, few / many, much

Exercise 6
1 more girls than boys
2 as many boys as girls
3 fewer boys than girls
4 fewer students than
5 more students than

Speaking

Exercise 1
A computer science   C mathematics
B engineering   D medicine

Exercise 2
1 medicine, lectures, doctor

2 course, interesting, director
3 law, difficult, lawyer

Exercise 3
business: 2   mathematics: 4
literature: 3   university: 5

Exercise 4

1 [O o]	2 [O o o]	3 [o o O o]	4 [o o O o o]
business	literature	mathematics	university

Exercise 5

1 [O o]	2 [O o o]	3 [o o O o]	4 [o o O o o]
business	literature	mathematics	university
college	chemistry	engineering	
deadline	graduate	graduation	
lecture	history	presentation	
project	medicine		
	timetable		

Exercise 7
1 b   4 c   7 j   10 i
2 e   5 a   8 g
3 d   6 h   9 f

Exercise 8
1 results   4 presentations
2 university / college 5 essay
3 year

Exercise 9
a Lara   b Marcel   c Dee

Exercise 10
now

Exercise 11
1 I'm revising for an exam. It's my final year and I'm working very hard. I'm having extra tuition and my grades are improving.

2 I'm visiting my brother at college. He's living in halls this year and he's having a great time. I'm helping him with his coursework this semester, and we're preparing a presentation at the moment.

3 I'm thinking about doing another course next year. I'm applying for a scholarship at a university in my hometown and I'm filling out the application form now.

Reading

Exercise 1
1 c   2 d   3 a   4 b

Exercise 2
1 RE (Religious Education)
2 numeracy
3 PE (Physical Education)
4 literacy

Exercise 4
1 nursery school   3 primary school
2 infant school   4 secondary school

5 6th form college **7** master's degree
6 bachelor's degree **8** PhD

Exercise 5
1 Japan		**9**	Heidelberg
2 Hanoi		**10**	Dutch
3 Vietnam		**11**	Maastricht
4 Kyoto		**12**	Dutch
5 Arabic		**13**	Brussels
6 Arab		**14**	German
7 Jeddah		**15**	Zurich
8 German			

Exercise 6
1 remember **3** remind **5** remind
2 remember **4** remember

Listening
Exercise 1
1 text books **3** exam hall
2 test **4** revision

Exercise 2
+ 'r': 7 later
+ 'er': 1 faster **3** cleverer **6** slower
y + 'ier': 8 healthier
'more' + adjective: 2 more interesting **4** more nervous
irregular adjectives: 5 better **9** worse **10** better

Exercise 3
2 B		**5** A		**8** E
3 C		**6** A		**9** E
4 B		**7** D		

Exercise 4
Suggested answers
1 better **4** slower
2 better / healthier **5** more nervous
3 more interesting

Exercise 5
1 intelligent, correctly **4** unusually, good
2 well, effectively **5** extraordinarily, high
3 fairly, quickly

Unit 8 Work Listening

Exercise 1
1 B **2** D **3** A **4** C

Exercise 2
1 businessman **3** doctor
2 police officer **4** farmer

Exercise 3
1 produce **4** earn
2 supply, deliver **5** trade
3 defend, guard **6** take care of

Exercise 4
1 look for **4** look over
2 look after **5** look through
3 look at

Exercise 5
1 look through **4** looked at
2 look for **5** look after
3 look over

Speaking
Exercise 1
1 businessman **6** police officer
2 chef **7** personal assistant
3 journalist **8** teacher
4 lawyer **9** volunteer
5 nurse

Exercise 2
A lawyer **C** personal assistant
B journalist **D** chef

Exercise 3
1 police officer **4** volunteer
2 journalist **5** businessman
3 nurse **6** teacher

Exercise 7
1 b **2** a **3** c **4** b, c

Exercise 8
a part-time, applied, earning
b company, work experience, use my languages, flexible hours
c help people, travel the world, earning a good salary

Exercise 10
1 have to **5** have to
2 had to **6** have to
3 didn't have to **7** don't have to
4 don't have to **8** have to

Exercise 13
1 as **3** for **5** use
2 to **4** well known **6** well paid

Reading
Exercise 1
1 slogan **3** logo
2 sign **4** advertisement

Exercise 2
Suggested answers
It's impossible to avoid <u>advertisements</u>. In our homes, <u>newspaper</u>, <u>magazine</u> and <u>television</u> <u>ads</u> compete for our attention. <u>Posters</u>, <u>billboards</u> and <u>flyers</u> greet us the moment we walk out the door. Advertising agencies stay busy thinking up new ways to get our attention. We have company <u>logos</u> on our clothes. Our <u>email</u> is full of <u>spam</u>, and <u>pop-ups</u> slow us down as we surf the Web. <u>Product placements</u> sneak into films and TV shows. '<u>Ad wrapping</u>' turns cars into moving <u>signboards</u>. Advertisers have even tried advertising in <u>TV commercials</u> in a subliminal way (affecting your mind without you knowing it). It's no wonder that this is called the consumer age.

Exercise 3
1 spam **5** signboards
2 product placement **6** consumer
3 billboards **7** pop-up
4 flyer

Exercise 4
2 magazine **5** company **8** consumer
3 television **6** product
4 advertising **7** TV

Exercise 5
1 web **2** website **3** focus

4 individuals **6** comments
5 corporation **7** activity

Exercise 6
1 A **2** an **3** a **4** the **5** the

Writing
Exercise 1
1 d / b **2** f **3** b **4** a **5** c
6 e

Exercise 2
Suggested answers
1 (In addition,) sitting at a desk in front of a computer all day can cause long-term back problems.
2 (Furthermore,) it enables people to work more quickly.
3 (Also,) social networking can occasionally be dangerous.

Exercise 3
Suggested answers
1 (yet) if companies encourage workers to follow health and safety regulations properly, these problems can be avoided.
2 (However,) technology at work can also mean that people spend too much time on the Internet or chatting online with friends.
3 (On the other hand,) social networking can make it easier to stay in touch with friends.

Exercise 4
1 Technology is a good thing because it helps people communicate more easily also. Also, it helps people do their jobs more efficiently.
2 People should always pay for music and not download it illegally. Downloading illegally is bad for the music industry. In addition, it is bad for musicians.
3 Computers have some negative points. It is not always easy to fix a computer if it goes wrong. However / On the other hand, there are lots of people who can fix computers.
4 Mobile phones can be dangerous if they are used in a car. In addition / Also / Furthermore / Moreover, they can be dangerous for pedestrians who use them when crossing the road.

Unit 9 Holidays and travel
Speaking

Exercise 1
A beach holiday **C** activity holiday
B coach tour **D** safari

Exercise 2
do: lessons or a course, new sports, sightseeing, water sports
eat in: traditional restaurants
go: sightseeing, swimming in the sea
go on: day trips
learn: new sports, water sports
take: day trips, lessons or a course, photos
visit: historical sites, tourist attractions, traditional restaurants
watch: local festivals, new sports, water sports

Exercise 4
1 d **2** f **3** e **4** c **5** b **6** a

Exercise 5
Possible answers
1 beautiful
2 comfortable / modern
3 exciting
4 delicious
5 friendly / unfriendly
6 boring / friendly / unfriendly
7 uncomfortable

Exercise 6
Tick: 1 learn new sports, 2 take lessons, 5 visit local festivals, 6 eat in traditional restaurants, 7 go on day trips

Exercise 9
1 with stress
2 no stress

Exercise 11
1 I'm going to stay in a hotel.
2 I'm not going to take any photos.
3 I'm going to eat in traditional restaurants.
4 We're going to visit historical sites.
5 We're not going to learn a new sport.
6 We're going to go sightseeing.

Writing

Exercise 1
1 (to increase,) to rise, to go up
2 to fall, to decrease, to go down, to drop
3 to remain stable, to stay the same
4 to fluctuate

Exercise 2
1 an increase
2 rose
3 decreased
4 a fall
5 went down
6 a drop
7 fluctuated

Exercise 4
1 rapid increase / sharp rise / rapid rise
2 fluctuated
3 sharp drop / sharp fall / sharp decrease / rapid drop / rapid fall / rapid decrease
4 rose sharply / rose rapidly / increased sharply / increased rapidly

Exercise 5
1 and 2 for 3 between / in 4 from

Listening

Exercise 1
A Japan
B Malaysia
C United Arab Emirates (UAE)
D Portugal

1 Venezuela, Venezuelan
2 Iran, Iranian
3 Finland, Finnish
4 Vietnam, Vietnamese
5 Yemen, Yemeni

Exercise 2
1 Japanese
2 Chinese
3 Egyptian
4 Emirati
5 Portuguese
6 Malaysian

Exercises 3 and 4
1 4.50
2 Beijing / China
3 UAE1880
4 Lisbon / Portugal
5 16

Reading

Exercise 1
1 motorway
2 dual carriageway
3 country lane
4 path

Exercise 2
1 motorway
2 path
3 dual carriageway
4 country lane

Exercise 3
commuter101 Is anybody else fed up with (roadworks)? Is it just here in London where they are appearing all at once, or is it the same everywhere? It's added an hour to my (journey). EACH WAY.

Heather98 Pretty much the same here, (commuter) 101. I have to do (a round trip) of 20 miles between Cheltenham and Birmingham every day and pass (very slowly!) 3 areas with (roadworks) on different parts of (the M5.) It's doubling the time it takes me to get to and from work.

Musicfan2 Take a (train) guys. Last time I checked, (trains) were going regularly between Cheltenham and Birmingham. And in London you've got (the) (Tube.)

CharlotteL. It's driving me crazy too. There are (roadworks) near the (service station) by (Junction 9) on (the M6.) It's like the traffic is at a standstill there. I try to avoid it but it's not always possible.

Heather98 @ Musicfan2: Not an option, I'm afraid. I am a sales rep and need my (car) during the day.

chico I agree with Musicfan. Instead of complaining about (roadworks) the cost of (petrol,) the price of (cars) etc. we need to think about other options. And I don't mean (car sharing) or building more motorways. I say we try to save our environment by campaigning for better (bus and) (train networks) and for different types of (public) (transport) such as (trams.) Use your time and anger to try and make a difference!

commuter101 What time? I'm stuck in (a traffic) (jam!!) (☺)

Exercise 4
1 fed up (with)
2 pretty much
3 round trip
4 M5, M6
5 service station
6 a junction
7 standstill
8 rep
9 campaigning

Exercise 5

Formal or neutral	Informal
to commute	to be fed up
almost	pretty much
a campaign	a rep
options	guys
anger	
a junction	

Exercise 6
1 c 2 b 3 d 4 a

Unit 10 Health Listening

Exercise 1
1 potatoes
2 bananas
3 cabbage
4 turkey
5 beef
6 cherries
7 cheese
8 butter
9 lamb
10 carrots
11 pineapple
12 yoghurt

Exercise 2

Meat	Dairy products	Vegetables	Fruit
turkey	cheese	potatoes	bananas
beef	butter	cabbage	cherries
lamb	yoghurt	carrots	pineapple

Exercise 3
2 U	8 C/U	14 C/U
3 C/U	9 C	15 C
4 C	10 C/U	16 U
5 U	11 U	17 C/U
6 C/U	12 U	18 C/U
7 U	13 C/U	

Exercise 5
1 d 3 a 5 i 7 j 9 b
2 j 4 h 6 e 8 c 10 f

Exercise 4
1.3 kg / kilograms of flour
10 *grams* of salt
300 g / grams of sugar
2 l / litres of milk
450 ml / millilitres of cooking oil

Exercise 6
1 ¾
2 two thirds
3 five eighths
4 ⅞

Exercise 7
1 ½ kilo – 500 g
2 250 g – ¼ kilo
3 330 g – ⅓ kilo
4 200 g – ⅕ kilo
5 ⅕ – 200 ml

Speaking

Exercise 1
A sleep for eight hours every night
B do sports
C eat well
D play board games

Exercise 2
Suggested answers

Good for your mind	Good for your body	Good for both
play board games	do sports, eat well	do sports
draw pictures	do taekwondo	sleep for eight hours every night
play a musical instrument	have a healthy diet	do yoga
play brain training games	play table tennis	

Exercise 3
1 doing yoga
2 brain training games
3 on my own
4 important to
5 makes me feel
6 good for

Exercise 5
Charles like playing chess with his father.
Rosa likes cooking for her family and friends.

Exercise 6
1 hard
2 keep your mind active
3 happy

Exercise 7
1 It's challenging / great / healthy / interesting / relaxing.
2 It's important to keep fit / relax after college / work in a team.
3 It makes me feel great / healthy / relaxed.

Exercise 9
1 It's	3 It's	5 shouldn't	
2 isn't	4 It's		

Exercise 11
1 shouldn't	3 should	5 should	
2 should	4 shouldn't	6 shouldn't	

Reading

Exercise 1
1 club   2 racket   3 bat   4 board

Exercise 2
Possible answers
racket: tennis, badminton, squash
board: snowboarding, skateboarding, surfing, windsurfing, snow-kiting, kitesurfing
bat: baseball, cricket, table tennis, rounders, softball

Exercise 3
1 golf
2 badminton
3 windsurfing
4 cricket

Suggested answers
water polo: a game played in a swimming pool between two teams in which the players try to score points by throwing the ball into a net
basketball: a game played between two teams in which players try to score points by throwing the ball through a hoop
netball: a game similar to basketball played between two teams of women in which players try to score points by throwing the ball through a hoop
tennis: a game played by two or four players in which the players use a racket to hit a ball over a net
swimming: a sport in which a person moves through the water using both their arms and their legs

Exercise 4
Pleasant / Positive feelings: amazed, amused, calm, confident, curious, delighted, excited, glad, happy, relaxed, wonderful
Unpleasant / Negative feelings: afraid, angry, annoyed, anxious, ashamed, bored, depressed, disappointed, embarrassed, frightened, guilty, jealous, miserable, nervous, sad, terrible, tired

Exercise 5
Possible answers
1 tired
2 amusing
3 disappointing
4 relaxed
5 depressing
6 exciting
7 frightening
8 embarrassed

Writing

Exercise 1
A doctor
B hospital
C medicine
D patient

Exercise 2
1 overweight   3 exercise   5 illness
2 junk food   4 cure   6 medicines

Exercise 3
1 b   2 a   3 c

Exercise 4
1 If junk food didn't exist, people wouldn't be overweight.
2 People would live longer if all diseases were cured.
3 If hospitals were free, more people would live longer.
4 If there were no doctors, there would be a lot more illness.

Unit 11 Taking responsibility
Reading

Exercise 1
A group of people: committee, council
A person: secretary, representative, member, chairperson
An object: minutes (of a minute)
An activity: election, voting, nomination

Exercise 2
1 Committee / Council
2 Minutes
3 election
4 chairperson
5 nominations
6 member / representative
7 voting / election

Exercise 3
1 council
2 committee
3 secretary
4 minutes
5 chairperson

Exercise 4
1 the photographs of the people partying on the beach with my sisters
2 the importance of the education I received in the UK
3 the details of the cases involving the teenagers who travelled without passports
4 the secret of a successful career

Writing

Exercise 1
1 (rush hour,) traffic jams
2 commute, crowded
3 fare, service
4 abroad, pollution

2 B   3 D   4 C

Exercise 2
1 to increase
2 travelling
3 finding
4 to travel
5 raising
6 to change
7 to see
8 to commute

Exercise 3
2 decided to walk
3 choose / chose to walk
4 appear to feel
5 to resist using

Exercise 4
2 Pollution
3 Public transport
4 Cars
5 a passport
6 the Internet

Speaking

Exercise 1
A graduating from university
B getting married
C travelling on your own for the first time
D winning a sports competition

Exercise 2
1 travelling on his own for the first time
2 his parents
3 very nervous, very excited

Exercise 4
Negative	Positive
bored / boring	delighted
terrified / terrifying	excited / exciting
tired / tiring	relaxed / relaxing
	satisfied / satisfying
	surprised / surprising

Exercise 5
Circle: terrified, boring, tired, surprised, relaxed, tiring, delighted, satisfied, exciting

Exercise 6
1 terrified   4 surprised   7 delighted
2 boring   5 relaxed   8 satisfied
3 tired   6 tiring   9 exciting

Exercise 7
1 very   2 really   3 very   4 really

Exercise 9
1 c   2 d   3 a   4 b

Exercise 10
1 most   4 more   7 more
2 more   5 most
3 better than   6 happier

Exercise 12
1 the   4 wasn't   7 than
2 younger   5 boring   8 felt
3 nervous   6 happier

Listening

Exercise 1
Suggested answers
A stress   C study
B deadline   D relaxation

Exercise 2
1 hobby   3 comfort   5 worker
2 work   4 beach   6 start

Exercise 3
Noun	Noun and verb
career	rest
job	work
hobby	stress

profession	worry
occupation	pressure
relaxation	comfort
leisure	shop
holidays	boss
difficulty	limit
factory	target
beach	start
office	
workshop	
employer	
owner	
worker	
manager	
deadline	
goal	

Exercise 4
1 job   **3** worry   **5** owner
2 holidays   **4** office   **6** deadline

Exercise 5
1 New York is not the capital of the United States of America.
2 In the UK, children who are born in July usually start school in September, just after they are five.
3 Oxford University is one of the most famous in the world.
4 In some countries, most companies close on Sundays, but in others they close on Fridays or Saturdays.
5 The official language of Greece is Greek.

Unit 12 Money Listening

Exercise 1
A 2   **B** 1   **C** 4   **D** 3

Exercise 2
1 customer services   **4** shopping malls
2 designer brands   **5** market stalls
3 self-service   **6** shop assistant

Exercise 3
1 I bought this shirt in a <u>sale</u>.
2 My <u>brother</u> thinks <u>online</u> shopping is much <u>quicker</u> than going to the <u>shops</u>.
3 The <u>good</u> thing about shopping in a <u>department</u> store is that you can get <u>everything</u> in <u>one</u> place.

---

4 The <u>last</u> time I took something back to a shop, the customer <u>services</u> manager wasn't <u>there</u>.
5 I <u>lost</u> my <u>credit</u> card the other day. I was really <u>worried</u> someone <u>else</u> would use it.
6 Have you ever bought a train ticket with a student <u>discount</u>? It's <u>so</u> much <u>cheaper</u>.

Exercise 4
1 d   **2** e   **3** b   **4** a   **5** c

Exercise 5
1 go shopping   **4** goes shopping
2 (shopping) list   **5** a refund
3 (the) supermarket

Speaking

Exercise 2
Possible answers
A (guitar): large, new, modern, wood
B (mobile phone): black, glass, metal, modern, plastic, small
C (painting): old-fashioned, gold, wood
D (bag): large, leather, old-fashioned

Exercise 3

Size	Age	Colour	Material
large	modern	green	glass
small	new	black	leather
	old-fashioned	gold	metal
		red	plastic
			gold
			wood

Exercise 4
1 electric guitar: expensive, modern, red, white, wood, plastic
2 handbag: large, old-fashioned, red, leather, beautiful

Exercise 6
1 e   **2** c   **3** a   **4** f   **5** b   **6** d

Exercise 7
1 I use it for
2 It reminds me of
3 It's important to me because
4 it's made of

Exercise 11
1 had, for
2 owned, since
3 used, for
4 carried, since
5 worn, for
6 wanted, since

Exercise 13
1 possessions   **4** had   **7** important
2 favourite   **5** bought   **8** reminds
3 it   **6** modern   **9** wear

Writing

Exercise 1
wealth (N)   spend (V)   save (V)   rich (A)
possessions (N)   inherit (V)   salary (N)   tax (N, V)
poverty (V)   wealthy (A)   savings (N)   income (N)
2 savings   **5** wealthy
3 salary   **6** income
4 poverty   **7** possessions

Exercise 2
1 tax   **3** save   **5** spend
2 salary   **4** wealthy   **6** income

Exercise 3
2 it (Happiness), it (Happiness)
3 they (people)
4 It (Good weather)
5 They (Children)
6 This (inherit(ing) a lot from their parents), they (people who inherit a lot from their parents)

Exercise 4
1 These changes; <u>have</u> P
2 This approach; <u>is</u> S
3 These actions; <u>help</u> P
4 This problem; <u>is</u> S

Reading

Exercise 1
1 b   **3** d   **5** i   **7** g   **9** f
2 e   **4** a   **6** h   **8** c

Exercise 2
Saving money: investment, saving account
Borrowing money from the bank: credit card, loan, mortgage, overdraft, owe
Getting your own money from the bank: ATM, automatic teller machine, cash point, cheque, debit card, hole in the wall, withdrawal
Earning money: pay slip, salary
Paying money: cheque, credit card, debit card, fees, fines, purchase, rent

Exercise 3
Underline: ATM, automatic teller machine, cash point, hole in the wall

Exercise 4
1 ATM / automatic teller machine / cash point / hole in the wall
2 fine
3 fees
4 overdraft
5 mortgage

Exercise 5
1 a   **2** b

Punctuation guide

The apostrophe (')

Misusing or omitting the apostrophe is one of the most common punctuation errors.

Showing possession

The apostrophe (') is used to show that something belongs to someone. It is usually added to the end of a word and followed by an -s.

- **-'s** is added to the end of singular words.

    Hannah's book

- **-'s** is added to the end of plural words not ending in -s.

    children's games

- An apostrophe alone (') is added to plural words ending in -s.

    Your grandparents are your parents' parents.

- **-'s** is added to the end of names and singular words ending in -s.

    James's car

- **-'s** is added to the end of certain professions or occupations to indicate workplaces.

    She's on her way to the doctor's.

- **-'s** is added to the end of people or their names to indicate that you are talking about their home.

    I'm going over to Harry's for tea tonight.

- Note that if the word is a classical Greek name, or a historical figure or building, an apostrophe only is sometimes preferred.

    Dickens' novels

- **-'s** can also be added to:
- whole phrases

    My next-door neighbour's dog was barking away like mad.

- indefinite pronouns such as somebody or anywhere

    Is this anybody's pencil case?

- each other

    We kept forgetting each other's names.

When the possessor is an inanimate object (rather than a living thing), the apostrophe is not used and the word order is changed.

> *the middle of the street (not the street's middle)*

To test whether an apostrophe is in the right place, think about who the owner is.

> *the boy's books [= the books belonging to the boy]*
>
> *the boys' books [= the books belonging to the boys]*

- Note that an apostrophe is *not* used to form possessive pronouns such as *its, yours,* or *theirs.*

- An apostrophe is *not* used to form the plurals of words such as *potatoes* or *tomatoes.*

With letters and numbers

An apostrophe is used in front of two figures referring to a year or decade.

> *French students rioted in '68 [short for '1968'].*
>
> *He worked as a schoolteacher during the '60s and early '90s.*

An apostrophe can be used in plurals of letters and numbers to make them more readable.

> *His 2's look a bit like 7's.*
>
> *She got straight A's in her exams.*

- Note that:

    it's = it is, e.g. *It's a holiday today.*

    its = belonging to it, e.g. *The dog was scratching its ear.*

Contracted forms

An apostrophe is used in shortened forms of words to show that one or more letters have been missed out. Contractions are usually shortened forms of auxiliary verbs

be	**have**
I'm	*I/we/they'**ve*** (have)
*We/you/they'**re*** (are)	*He/she/it/one'**s*** (has)
*He/she/it/one'**s*** (is)	*I/we/you/he/she/it/one/*
	*they'**d*** (had)

would

*I/we/you/he/she/it/one/they'**d*** (would)

or the negative not.

not

*We/you/they are**n't***

*He/she/it/one is**n't***

*I/we/they have**n't***

*He/she/it/one has**n't***

In order to work out what the contracted forms **'s** and **'d** represent, you need to look at what follows it:

– If **'s** is followed by an *-ing* form, it represents the auxiliary *is*.

> *She'**s reading** a book about the ancient Egyptians.*

– If **'s** is followed by an adjective or a noun phrase, it represents the main verb *is*.

> *She'**s nervous** about meeting my parents.*

– If **'s** is followed by a past participle, it can represent *is* as it is used in the passive,

> *He'**s portrayed** by the media as a kindly old grandfather.*

or *has* as it is used in the present perfect.

> *She'**s broken** her wrist.*

– If **'s** is followed by *got*, it represents the auxiliary *has*.

> *She'**s got** two brothers and one sister.*

– If **'d** is followed by a past participle, it represents the auxiliary *had*.

> *She couldn't believe what she'**d done**.*

– If **'d** is followed by a base form, it represents the modal auxiliary *would*.

> *I'**d give up** now, if I were you.*

– If **'d** is followed by *rather* or *better*, it represents the modal auxiliary *would*.

> *We'**d better** go home soon.*
>
> *I'**d rather** not talk about that.*

The comma (,)

The comma marks a short pause between elements in a sentence.

Separating main clauses

Main clauses that are joined together with *and* or *but* do not normally have a comma before the conjunction unless the two clauses have different subjects.

> *You go out of the door and turn immediately left.*
>
> *It was cold outside, but we decided to go out for a walk anyway.*

Separating subordinate clauses from main clauses

Commas are normally used if the subordinate clause comes before the main clause.

> *If you have any problems, just call me.*
>
> *Just call me if you have any problems.*

Sometimes a comma is used even when the main clause comes first, if the clauses are particularly long.

> *We should be able to finish the work by the end of the week, if nothing unexpected turns up between now and then.*

Separating relative clauses from main clauses

Commas are used to mark off non-defining relative clauses. This is the type of clause that adds to information about a noun or noun phrase.

> *My next-door neighbour, who works from home, is keeping an eye on the house while we're away.*
>
> *She moved to Los Angeles, where she was immediately signed as a singer songwriter.*

Commas are not required in defining relative clauses, since these simply postmodify the noun.

> *Let's make sure the money goes to the people **who need it most**.*
>
> *The computer **(that) I borrowed** kept on crashing.*

Separating items in a list

Commas are used to separate three or more items in a list or series.

> *She got out bread, butter, and jam (but bread and butter).*

• Note that the comma is often not given before the final *and* or *or*.

> *They breed dogs, cats, rabbits and hamsters.*

Separating adjectives

Commas are used between adjectives, whether they come before the noun or after a linking verb.

> *It was a hot, dry and dusty road.*
>
> *It's wet, cold and windy outside.*

A comma is not usually used before an adjective that is followed by *and*.

With adverbials

When an adverbial such as *however, therefore* or *unfortunately* modifies a whole sentence, it is separated from the rest of the sentence by a comma.

> *Therefore, I try to avoid using the car as much as possible.*

With question tags and short responses

Commas are used before question tags and after *yes* or *no* in short responses.

> *It's quite cold today, isn't it?*
>
> *You're Amy Osborne, aren't you? – No, I'm not.*

With vocatives

Commas are used to separate the name of a person or group being addressed from the rest of the sentence.

> *Come on, Olivia, be reasonable.*
>
> *Dad, can you come and help me, please?*

With discourse markers

Commas are used to separate discourse markers like Well and Now then from the rest of the sentence.

> *Well, believe it or not, I actually passed!*
>
> *Actually, I quite enjoyed it.*

In reported speech

Commas are used to follow direct speech (if there is no question or exclamation mark after the quotation), or to show that it comes next.

> *'I don't understand this question,' said Peter.*
>
> *'You're crazy!' Claire exclaimed.*

In dates

A comma must be used between the day of the month and the year, when the two numbers are next to each other.

> *March 31, 2011*

Quotation marks (' ') or (" ")

Direct speech

Direct speech gives the actual words that a speaker used. It is common in novels and other writing where the actual words of a speaker are quoted.

The words spoken are enclosed in single or double quotation marks.

> **'Have you been to the new shopping precinct yet?'** *enquired Shona.*
>
> **"I've already seen it,"** *John replied.*

- The comma comes inside the quotation marks, unless the reporting verb is positioned inside a reported sentence that itself does not require a comma.

> *'There is', Monica said, 'nothing we can do about it.'*

Other uses

Single quotation marks are sometimes used:

- to draw attention to a word

> *The word **'book'** can be used as a noun or a verb.*

- to indicate an unusual use of a word

> *She pointed out that websites used for internet voting could be **'spoofed'**.*

Capital letters

A capital (or 'upper case') letter is used to mark the beginning of a sentence.

> **W**hen I was 20, I dropped out of university and became a model.

Capital letters are also used for the first letter in proper nouns. These include:

- people's names

> **J**enny **F**orbes

- days of the week

> **W**ednesday

- months of the year

> **A**ugust

- public holidays

> **C**hristmas

- nationalities

> **S**panish

- languages

> **S**wahili

- geographical locations

> **A**ustralia
>
> **T**he **M**editerranean **S**ea

- company names

> **D**yson

- religions

> **I**slam

Capital letters are also used for the first letter in titles of books, magazines, newspapers, TV shows, films, etc. Where there are several words, a capital letter is usually used for all the main content words in the title (i.e. not the prepositions or the determiners – unless they are the first word in the title).

The **T**imes

Twelfth **N**ight   **T**he **S**ecret **G**arden

The full stop (.)

Full stops are used:

– to mark the end of a sentence

I have to catch a bus in ten minutes.

– to mark the end of a sentence fragment

Do you like this sort of music? Not really.

– in initials for people's names, although this practice is becoming less frequent

J.K. Rowling   *Iain M. Banks*

– after abbreviations, although this practice is becoming less frequent.

P.S. Do pop in next time you're passing.

She's moved to the I.T. department

When an abbreviation consists of a shortened word such as Re. or Prof., a full stop is needed.

Prof. John Johansson will be speaking on the subject of 'Discourse in the Electronic Age'.

When an abbreviation contains the last letter of the shortened word, a full stop is not needed.

***Dr** McDonald*

*41, Douglas **Rd***

• Note that full stops are not used in many common sets of initials,

*Did you see that programme on **BBC** 2 last night?*

or at the end of headlines, headings and titles.

Fear grips global stock markets

Wuthering Heights

Remember that a full stop, and not a question mark, is used after an indirect question or a polite request.

He asked if the bus had left.

The question mark (?)

The question mark marks the end of a question.

*When will we be arriving**?***

Question marks are used in direct questions, i.e. when the actual words of a speaker are used. A reported question should end with a full stop.

*The lady said, 'Where are you going**?**'*

The lady asked where she was going.

• Note that you put a question mark at the end of a question, even if the words in the sentence are not in the normal question order, or some words are omitted. Care is needed here as such a sentence can look, at first sight, like a statement rather than a question.

*You know he doesn't live here any longer**?***

A full stop, rather than a question mark, is used after an indirect question.

*I'd like to know what you've been doing all this time**.***

A full stop also replaces a question mark at the end of a sentence which looks like a question if, in fact, it is really a polite request.

Will you please return the completed forms to me.

The exclamation mark (!)

The exclamation mark is used after exclamations and emphatic expressions.

*I can't believe it**!***

*Oh, no! Look at this mess**!***

• The exclamation mark loses its effect if it is overused. It is better to use a full stop after a sentence expressing mild excitement or humour.

It was such a beautiful day.

I felt like a perfect banana.

The colon (:)

The colon indicates a break between two main clauses which is stronger than a comma but weaker than a full stop.

A colon is used:

– in front of a list

*I used three colours**:** green, blue and pink.*

– in front of an explanation or a reason

*I decided against going away this weekend**:** the weather forecast was dreadful.*

– after introductory headings

*Start time**:** 10 o'clock.*

- in more formal writing, between two main clauses that are connected

    Be patient: the next book in the series has not yet been published.

- in front of the second part of a book title

    Farming and wildlife: a study in compromise

- to introduce direct speech, especially in American English, or when the quotation is particularly long.

    He said: 'You owe me three dollars and twenty-five cents.'

The semicolon (;)

The semicolon is used to mark a break between two main clauses when there is a balance or a contrast between the clauses.

    Compare:

    The engine roared into life. The propellers began to turn.

    The plane taxied down the runway ready for takeoff.

    with:

    The engine roared into life; the propellers began to turn; the plane taxied down the runway ready for takeoff.

A useful test to work out when to use a semicolon is to ask yourself whether the two clauses could be written instead as separate sentences. If the answer is 'yes', then you can use a semicolon.

- Note that it is quite acceptable to use a full stop in these cases, but a semicolon is preferable if you wish to convey the sense of a link or continuity between the clauses in your narrative.

    I'm not that interested in jazz; I prefer classical music.

A semicolon is also used to separate items in a list, especially if the listed items are phrases or clauses, which may already contain commas.

    The holiday was a disaster: the flight was four hours late; the hotel, which was described as 'luxury', was dirty; and it rained for the whole fortnight.

Brackets ( )

Brackets (also called **parentheses**) are used to enclose a word or words which can be left out and still leave a meaningful sentence.

This is a process which Hayek (a writer who came to rather different conclusions) also observed.

Brackets are also used to show alternatives or options.

    Any student(s) interested in taking part should e-mail me.

- Note that when the structure of the sentence as a whole demands punctuation after a bracketed section, the punctuation is given outside the brackets.

    I haven't yet spoken to John (I mean John Maple, my boss), but I have a meeting with him on Friday.

Punctuation is given before the closing brackets only when it applies to the bracketed section rather than to the sentence as a whole.

    It's cold today (absolutely freezing in fact!).

Square brackets [ ]

Square brackets are used, usually in books and articles, when supplying words that make a quotation clearer or that comment on it, although they were not originally said or written.

    Mr Runcie concluded: 'The novel is at its strongest when describing the dignity of Cambridge [a slave] and the education of Emily [the daughter of an absentee landlord].'

The hyphen (-)

The hyphen joins words or parts of words.

Hyphens are used at the ends of lines where a word has been split, to warn the reader that the word continues on the next line. If the word you need to split is clearly made up of two or more smaller words or elements, you should put the hyphen after the first of these parts. Otherwise, you put the hyphen at the end of a syllable.

    wheel-barrow   *inter-national*

    infor-mation

It is best not to add a hyphen if the word is a short one, or if it would mean writing just one or two letters at the end or beginning of a line. For example, it would be better to write 'unnatural' on the line below, rather than writing 'un-' on one line and 'natural' on the next.

Prefixes that are used in front of a word beginning with a capital letter always have a hyphen after them.

    a wave of anti-British feeling

    a neo-Byzantine cathedral

A hyphen is used to join two or more words that together form an adjective, where this adjective is used *before* the noun it describes.

> *an up-to-date account*
>
> *a last-minute rush*
>
> *a six-year-old boy*

The hyphen is omitted when the adjective so formed comes after the noun or pronoun it describes.

> *The accounts are up to date.*
>
> *It was all rather last minute.*
>
> *He's six years old.*

Some common compound nouns are usually written with hyphens.

> *mother-in-law*   *great-grandmother*

Hyphens can be used to split words that have been formed by adding a prefix to another word, especially to avoid an awkward combination of letters or confusion with another word.

> *re-elect*

The dash (–)

A spaced dash (i.e. with a single space before and after it) is used:

– at the beginning and end of a comment that interrupts the flow of a sentence.

> *Now children – Kenneth, stop that immediately! – open your books on page 20.*

– to separate off extra information.

> *Boots and shoes – all shapes, sizes and colours – tumbled out.*

An unspaced dash (i.e. with no space before or after it) is used:

– to indicate a range.

> *pages 26–42*

– between two adjectives or noun modifiers that indicate that two countries or groups are involved in something or that an individual has two roles or aspects.

> *Swedish–Norwegian relations*
>
> *a mathematician–philosopher*

– to indicate that something such as a plane or a train goes between two places.

> *the New York–Montreal train*

The slash (/)

The slash separates letters, words or numbers. It is used to indicate alternatives, ratios and ranges, and in website addresses.

> *he/she/it*
>
> *200 km/hr*
>
> *the 2001/02 accounting year*
>
> *http://www.abcdefg.com*

Punctuation in numbers

Dates

Full stops or slashes are often used in dates.

	American usage
12.3.09	*3/12/09*
2.28.15	*2/28/15*

Scientific usage

Full stops are not used in scientific abbreviations.

> *12 kg*   *50 cm*

Times

Full stops and occasionally colons are used in times.

4.15 p.m.	*21.15*
3:30 a.m.	*20:30*

Long numbers

Commas are used in numbers to mark off units of thousands and millions.

> *1,359*   *2,543,678*

Decimals

Full stops indicate decimal points.

> *1.5*   *25.08*

Pronunciation guide

In this book the International Phonetic Alphabet (IPA) is used to show how some words are pronounced. The symbols used in the International Phonetic Alphabet are shown in the table below.

IPA Symbols

Vowel	Sounds	Consonant	Sounds
ɑ	calm, ah	b	bed, rub
æ	act, cat	d	done, red
aɪ	dive, cry	f	fit, if
aɪə	fire, tyre	g	good, dog
aʊ	out, down	h	hat, horse
aʊə	flour, sour	j	yellow, you
e	met, lend, pen	k	king, pick
eɪ	say, weight	l	lip, bill
eə	fair, care	m	mat, jam
ɪ	fit, win	n	not, tin
i	seem, me	p	pay, lip
ɪə	near, beard	r	run, read
ɒ	lot, spot	s	soon, bus
əʊ	note, coat	t	talk, bet
ɔ	raw, more	v	van, love
ɔɪ	boy, joint	w	win, wool
ʊ	could, stood	x	loch
u	you, use	z	zoo, buzz
ʊə	cure, pure	ʃ	ship, wish
ɜ	turn, third	ʒ	measure, television
ʌ	fund, must	ŋ	sing, working
ə	about	tʃ	cheap, witch
		θ	thin, earth
ː	lengthens the vowel sound	ð	then, bathe
		dʒ	joy, bridge